# Sri La

# Everything You Need
# to Know

# Introduction to Sri Lanka

Sri Lanka, a captivating island nation nestled in the Indian Ocean, offers a wealth of cultural, historical, and natural wonders that have long enchanted travelers from around the world. Its rich tapestry of heritage, stunning landscapes, and warm hospitality make it a unique destination that beckons explorers and adventurers alike.

Geographically positioned off the southern tip of India, Sri Lanka, formerly known as Ceylon, boasts a diverse topography that ranges from lush tropical forests to pristine beaches, rolling hills, and soaring mountains. Its compact size, roughly resembling a teardrop, belies the sheer variety of experiences that await those who venture onto its shores.

Sri Lanka's history is as compelling as its landscapes. The island's chronicles date back over 2,500 years, making it one of the oldest recorded civilizations in South Asia. It was once home to several ancient kingdoms, most notably the Sinhalese and Tamil kingdoms, which left behind a legacy of architectural marvels, religious sites, and a rich cultural heritage.

Buddhism, introduced to Sri Lanka in the 3rd century BCE, has played a pivotal role in shaping the island's identity. The iconic ancient city of Anuradhapura, with its sprawling monastic complexes and colossal stupas, stands as a testament to the enduring influence of Buddhism on Sri Lankan culture. In addition to its Buddhist heritage, Sri Lanka is a melting pot of religions and traditions. Hinduism, Islam, and Christianity coexist harmoniously with Buddhism, adding layers of diversity to the island's cultural mosaic. Each faith has its own sacred sites, festivals, and rituals that contribute to the vibrant tapestry of Sri Lankan life.

One cannot discuss Sri Lanka without mentioning its cuisine, which is an eclectic fusion of flavors and influences. From aromatic curries infused with spices to delectable sweets like "kavum" and "wattalappam," Sri Lankan food is a treat for the senses. And let's not forget the world-renowned Ceylon tea, which is grown in the island's central highlands and is celebrated for its exceptional quality.

Beyond the cultural and historical treasures, Sri Lanka's natural beauty is nothing short of breathtaking. The island is home to an astonishing array of wildlife, including leopards, elephants, and a dazzling variety of bird species. The lush rainforests of Sinharaja and the untamed wilderness of Yala National Park offer thrilling opportunities for wildlife enthusiasts and nature lovers.

Sri Lanka's coastline stretches for over 1,300 kilometers, offering pristine beaches that cater to all tastes. Whether you seek a quiet escape, thrilling water sports, or a chance to witness the majestic spectacle of whales and dolphins, the coastal regions of Sri Lanka have it all.

Throughout this book, we will embark on a journey through the heart of Sri Lanka, delving deeper into its history, culture, natural wonders, and the experiences it has to offer. Prepare to be captivated by this jewel of the Indian Ocean, a land where ancient traditions seamlessly blend with modern aspirations, creating a tapestry of stories waiting to be discovered.

# Geographical Wonders of Sri Lanka

Sri Lanka, the resplendent island in the Indian Ocean, is a geographical marvel that never ceases to amaze. From lush rainforests to towering mountains and pristine coastlines, this tropical paradise offers an astounding array of natural wonders that leave visitors spellbound.

Nestled within the island's heart lies the Central Highlands, where the terrain rises dramatically. Pidurutalagala, standing as Sri Lanka's tallest peak, reaches a staggering height of 8,281 feet (2,524 meters) above sea level. The landscape is an intricate patchwork of emerald tea plantations, rugged terrain, and cloud forests, creating an otherworldly vista that's home to an astonishing variety of flora and fauna.

Venture southward, and you'll find the verdant Sinharaja Forest Reserve, a UNESCO World Heritage Site that showcases the island's biodiversity at its finest. This pristine rainforest is a treasure trove of endemic species, including birds, reptiles, and countless plant varieties, some of which can't be found anywhere else on Earth. The lush canopy and murmuring streams of Sinharaja make it a haven for nature enthusiasts and researchers alike.

Sri Lanka's coastline, extending for more than 1,300 kilometers, boasts some of the world's most beautiful beaches. The golden sands of Bentota, the palm-fringed shores of Mirissa, and the serene coves of Trincomalee all offer their unique charm. And let's not forget the ethereal beaches of the Maldives, just a hop away from Sri Lanka's southwestern coast. As you make your way inland, the island's interior reveals a network of impressive rivers and cascading waterfalls. The Mahaweli River, the longest in Sri Lanka, meanders through picturesque landscapes, while waterfalls like Bambarakanda and Diyaluma captivate with their sheer beauty and plunging heights.

Now, shift your gaze to Sri Lanka's east, and you'll encounter the mesmerizing beauty of Arugam Bay, a world-renowned surfing destination. Surfers flock to its waves, and it's not just the surf that makes this spot special; the untouched lagoons and mangrove swamps offer an abundance of wildlife and tranquility.

In the north, the Jaffna Peninsula beckons with its unique geography. This region, separated from the rest of the island for decades due to conflict, is slowly opening up to reveal its hidden treasures. The vast lagoons, barren landscapes, and distinctive Hindu temples paint a different picture of Sri Lanka, one that showcases the island's diversity.

Lastly, let's not forget Sri Lanka's numerous islands, each with its own charm. Pigeon Island, located off the coast of Trincomalee, is a marine national park teeming with coral reefs and marine life. It's a snorkeler's paradise. Off the southern coast, you'll find Delft Island, known for its wild ponies and Dutch ruins, providing a fascinating glimpse into the island's colonial past.

Sri Lanka's geographical wonders are as diverse as they are captivating. From towering peaks to dense jungles, pristine beaches to meandering rivers, each corner of this island nation offers a unique natural experience that's bound to leave an indelible mark on any traveler fortunate enough to explore its riches.

# A Brief Overview of Sri Lankan History

The history of Sri Lanka is a tapestry woven with threads of ancient civilizations, kingdoms, colonization, and independence. Spanning over two millennia, it's a captivating journey through time that has shaped the island's rich cultural and historical identity.

The earliest records of human habitation in Sri Lanka date back to the Paleolithic era, with evidence of ancient tools and artifacts found in various regions. However, it's during the Iron Age that the island's history becomes more defined. Around 500 BCE, Indo-Aryan migrants settled on the island, bringing with them the foundation of what would later become Sinhalese culture and language.

The island's first major civilization, the Anuradhapura Kingdom, emerged in the 4th century BCE, centered in the north-central region. This kingdom played a pivotal role in the spread of Buddhism, with the arrival of Buddhism in Sri Lanka occurring during the reign of King Devanampiya Tissa.

The Anuradhapura Kingdom flourished for over a millennium, its monarchs overseeing the construction of grand stupas, monasteries, and a complex hydraulic system that harnessed the island's water resources. Among these architectural marvels is the Ruwanwelisaya, a massive stupa that still stands today as a testament to ancient Sri Lankan engineering and craftsmanship.

However, the kingdom faced challenges from invasions and internal conflicts, eventually leading to its decline. In the 9th century CE, the capital was moved to Polonnaruwa, marking the beginning of the Polonnaruwa Kingdom. This era saw the continuation of Buddhist art and culture but also witnessed periodic invasions, including those by the Cholas from South India.

The island's history took another dramatic turn with the arrival of European powers in the 16th century. The Portuguese were the first to establish a foothold, followed by the Dutch and eventually the British. Colonial rule, lasting for several centuries, left a profound impact on Sri Lanka, influencing its governance, culture, and society.

In 1948, Sri Lanka, then known as Ceylon, gained independence from British colonial rule. The country embarked on a path toward self-determination and nation-building. A significant milestone in its post-independence history was the adoption of a new constitution in 1972, which changed the country's name to the Democratic Socialist Republic of Sri Lanka and declared Sinhala as the official language.

Sri Lanka's recent history has been marked by periods of ethnic conflict and civil unrest, primarily between the Sinhalese majority and the Tamil minority. The conflict, which lasted for decades, resulted in significant social and political changes, including the devolution of power to provincial governments.

In more recent years, Sri Lanka has transitioned towards peace and reconciliation efforts, with the end of the civil war in 2009. The island has also focused on economic development and has become a popular destination for tourists seeking its natural beauty, rich heritage, and warm hospitality.

This brief overview of Sri Lankan history merely scratches the surface of a complex and multifaceted narrative. From ancient kingdoms to colonial rule and independence, the island's history is a story of resilience, cultural diversity, and the enduring spirit of its people.

# Ancient Civilizations and Archaeological Sites

Sri Lanka's history is a treasure trove of ancient civilizations and archaeological wonders that offer a glimpse into the past like no other. From the earliest known settlements to grand kingdoms, these sites hold the secrets of bygone eras.

One of the most iconic and ancient sites in Sri Lanka is Anuradhapura, dating back to the 4th century BCE. It was the capital of the first major kingdom on the island, the Anuradhapura Kingdom. This sprawling city boasted magnificent stupas, including the Ruwanwelisaya, as well as monastic complexes and intricate irrigation systems. The sacred Bodhi tree, believed to be a sapling of the tree under which Buddha attained enlightenment, is found here, making it a pilgrimage site for Buddhists worldwide.

Moving forward in time, Polonnaruwa, the second ancient capital of Sri Lanka, emerged in the 9th century CE. The ruins of Polonnaruwa reveal a rich history, with well-preserved structures like the Gal Vihara, a group of colossal Buddha statues carved into the rock, showcasing remarkable craftsmanship.

In the central highlands, the city of Sigiriya stands as a testament to ancient engineering and artistic prowess. This rock fortress, built by King Kasyapa in the 5th century CE, features a palace complex atop a towering rock and stunning frescoes that have survived for centuries. The view from the summit provides a breathtaking panorama of the surrounding countryside.

Venturing further back in history, the coastal town of Tissamaharama reveals remnants of an ancient Buddhist stupa dating to the 3rd century BCE. It's a serene site that showcases the enduring spiritual significance of the region.

Sri Lanka's cultural heritage is not confined to the mainland alone. The island of Anuradhapura, an ancient monastic complex located on an islet in the Tissa Wewa reservoir, preserves the ruins of a once-thriving monastic community. The serene surroundings and stone inscriptions provide insights into the island's monastic traditions.

On the northeastern coast, the ancient port city of Trincomalee has its own historical significance. It served as a crucial trading hub for various civilizations, including the Cholas, Pandya, and Portuguese. The Koneswaram Temple, perched on a promontory overlooking the sea, is a testament to the island's religious and cultural diversity.

As we journey through Sri Lanka's past, these archaeological sites offer a window into the island's rich and diverse history. From the grandeur of Anuradhapura to the artistic marvels of Sigiriya and the cultural tapestry of Trincomalee, each site tells a unique story of the people who once thrived in these ancient civilizations, leaving behind a legacy that continues to captivate and inspire.

# Colonial Influence on Sri Lanka

Sri Lanka's history bears the indelible marks of colonial influence, a period of transformation that left an enduring impact on the island's culture, society, and governance. From the arrival of the Portuguese in the early 16th century to the eventual departure of the British in the mid-20th century, Sri Lanka's colonial history is a complex narrative of conquest, trade, and cultural exchange.

The Portuguese were the first European power to establish a presence on the island in the early 1500s. Their arrival marked the beginning of a new era in Sri Lanka's history. They set up coastal forts and established control over several key ports, facilitating the expansion of their trade networks. This period also witnessed the introduction of Christianity, which made inroads among the local population.

In the 17th century, the Dutch ousted the Portuguese and took control of Sri Lanka's coastal regions, primarily for their strategic value in the lucrative spice trade. The Dutch influence was marked by the construction of impressive forts, such as Galle Fort, which stands as a testament to their architectural prowess. During this time, the Dutch also introduced new agricultural practices, including the cultivation of cash crops like cinnamon.

The British arrived in the late 18th century and gradually extended their influence over the island. They established a centralized administrative system, which included introducing English as the medium of instruction and implementing a legal framework that continues to shape Sri

Lanka's legal system to this day. The British also expanded the island's plantation economy, focusing on crops like tea, rubber, and coffee.

By the early 20th century, the struggle for independence had gained momentum, culminating in Sri Lanka's eventual attainment of independence in 1948. The island, then known as Ceylon, transitioned from British colonial rule to self-governance. This period marked the beginning of a new chapter in Sri Lanka's history, with the nation grappling with questions of identity, governance, and social justice.

The legacy of colonialism in Sri Lanka is complex. While it brought about modernization and infrastructure development, it also left behind scars of exploitation and social divisions. The influence of colonial languages, religions, and legal systems continues to shape contemporary Sri Lankan society.

Sri Lanka's colonial history is a testament to the resilience of its people and their ability to navigate the challenges of foreign rule. It's a story of transformation, resistance, and the eventual pursuit of self-determination that continues to shape the island nation's identity as it moves forward into the 21st century.

# Independence and Modern Sri Lanka

The story of modern Sri Lanka is a tale of nation-building, independence struggles, and the complexities of forging a unified identity. Emerging from the shadows of colonial rule, the island nation embarked on a journey of self-determination that has shaped its trajectory in the modern era.

On February 4, 1948, Ceylon, as it was then known, achieved independence from British colonial rule. The end of over four centuries of foreign domination marked a pivotal moment in the nation's history. A new era had dawned, and Ceylon was now free to chart its own course.

The early years of independence were marked by the formation of a democratic government under the leadership of Prime Minister D.S. Senanayake. The country chose a path of parliamentary democracy, inspired by the British system. Despite challenges, Ceylon managed to maintain political stability in its formative years.

One of the significant developments during this period was the adoption of a new constitution in 1947, which established Ceylon as a dominion within the British Commonwealth. This constitution also laid the foundation for the country's democratic institutions and legal framework. Sri Lanka's transition to independence was accompanied by efforts to address pressing social issues. Land reforms aimed to redistribute land to the landless, and education reforms expanded access to schooling for all. However, the nation still grappled with economic disparities and social inequalities inherited from its colonial

17

past. In 1956, a significant turning point occurred with the election of Solomon Bandaranaike as prime minister. His government pursued a policy of Sinhala nationalism, which led to the elevation of Sinhala as the sole official language and the promotion of Buddhist culture. This policy stirred ethnic tensions, particularly with the Tamil minority, and laid the groundwork for later conflicts.

In the decades that followed, Sri Lanka faced various challenges, including economic struggles, political instability, and a protracted civil conflict. The conflict between the government and the Liberation Tigers of Tamil Eelam (LTTE), a militant separatist group, lasted for nearly three decades and left a profound impact on the nation.

The conflict finally came to an end in 2009, following a military offensive by the government. While it brought an end to the violence, it also raised questions about reconciliation, justice, and the long-term prospects for peace.

In recent years, Sri Lanka has focused on post-conflict reconstruction, economic development, and strengthening its ties with the international community. The island nation's natural beauty, cultural heritage, and strategic location have made it an attractive destination for tourism and investment.

As Sri Lanka navigates the challenges of the modern era, it continues to grapple with issues of governance, reconciliation, and the preservation of its rich cultural diversity. The nation stands at a crossroads, poised to harness its potential and overcome the complex legacies of its past, as it marches forward into an uncertain but hopeful future.

# The People of Sri Lanka: Diversity and Demographics

Sri Lanka, often referred to as the "Pearl of the Indian Ocean," is a nation teeming with diversity, both in its people and its demographics. Situated at the crossroads of Asia, this island nation has a rich tapestry of ethnicities, cultures, and traditions that have evolved over centuries.

At the heart of Sri Lanka's population are the Sinhalese, who make up the majority of the island's inhabitants. They are predominantly Buddhist and have played a central role in shaping the nation's culture and identity. Sinhala is the official language of Sri Lanka, and many of the island's historical and religious sites are associated with Sinhalese heritage.

The Tamil community is the largest ethnic minority in Sri Lanka, primarily concentrated in the northern and eastern regions. They are predominantly Hindu and speak Tamil. The Tamil population has a distinct cultural and linguistic heritage, and their presence has contributed to the nation's rich diversity.

Muslims, who are mainly of Moor and Malay descent, represent another significant minority in Sri Lanka. They follow Islam and have made significant contributions to the country's commerce, culture, and cuisine. The Moor community, in particular, has a long history on the island and has played a pivotal role in trade and business.

Sri Lanka is also home to various indigenous groups, such as the Vedda people. These communities have their unique languages, traditions, and ways of life, often living in remote areas and maintaining a close connection with the natural world.

In addition to these major ethnic groups, Sri Lanka has a small but notable population of Burghers, who are of mixed European and Sri Lankan descent. They have a distinct cultural identity and have contributed to the country's artistic and culinary heritage.

The demographics of Sri Lanka extend beyond ethnicity to encompass religion, with Buddhism, Hinduism, Islam, and Christianity being the main faiths practiced on the island. Buddhism, with its deep historical roots, holds a central place in Sri Lankan society and culture.

The country's population is predominantly urban, with significant concentrations in cities like Colombo, Kandy, and Jaffna. Urbanization has led to changes in lifestyle and employment patterns, with a growing middle class and a dynamic economy that encompasses industries like tourism, manufacturing, and services.

Sri Lanka's population is characterized by its relatively high literacy rate and access to education. The government has invested in expanding educational opportunities, resulting in a well-educated workforce that contributes to the nation's development.

While the island's diversity is a source of strength and richness, it has also been a factor in the country's history of ethnic tensions and conflicts. The Sri Lankan government has made efforts to address these issues and promote reconciliation among its diverse communities.

As Sri Lanka moves forward in the 21st century, its demographics continue to evolve, shaped by globalization, urbanization, and changing social dynamics. The nation's commitment to preserving its cultural diversity while fostering unity remains a fundamental challenge and aspiration for its people, making the story of Sri Lanka's demographics an ongoing and compelling narrative.

# Languages Spoken in Sri Lanka

Sri Lanka, with its rich cultural tapestry and diverse ethnic groups, is a linguistic mosaic that reflects the island's complex history and heritage. The languages spoken in Sri Lanka are a testament to the nation's multicultural identity and the influence of various civilizations that have shaped its linguistic landscape over the centuries.

Sinhala is the official language of Sri Lanka and the mother tongue of the majority Sinhalese population. It is an Indo-Aryan language, written in a unique script known as Sinhala script. Sinhala is not only the primary language of communication but also plays a central role in the country's cultural and literary traditions. The language is known for its complex grammar and rich vocabulary.

Tamil, another significant language in Sri Lanka, is predominantly spoken by the Tamil ethnic community, particularly in the northern and eastern regions of the island. There are two main dialects of Tamil spoken in Sri Lanka: Jaffna Tamil and Batticaloa Tamil. The Tamil language has a long history on the island and is written in the Tamil script. It holds immense cultural and religious importance, particularly among Sri Lankan Tamils.

English also holds a prominent place in Sri Lanka, serving as a link language among different communities and an essential medium of instruction in education. Sri Lanka's colonial history under British rule left a lasting legacy, with English being widely used in business, government, and education. Many Sri Lankans are bilingual, with proficiency in both Sinhala or Tamil and English.

In addition to Sinhala, Tamil, and English, Sri Lanka is home to a multitude of other languages spoken by various communities. These include Malay, spoken by the Malay ethnic group, and Arabic, used by the Muslim community. There are also indigenous languages like Vedda, spoken by the Vedda people, an indigenous group living in remote areas of the island.

The linguistic diversity of Sri Lanka is a reflection of its multicultural society, with each language carrying its unique history, traditions, and cultural significance. While Sinhala and Tamil are the most widely spoken languages, the coexistence of multiple languages adds depth and richness to the island's identity.

Efforts have been made to promote multilingualism and preserve linguistic diversity in Sri Lanka. Language policies aim to ensure equal access to education and public services in both Sinhala and Tamil, fostering a sense of inclusivity and unity among the island's diverse communities.

The languages spoken in Sri Lanka are not just a means of communication but also a reflection of the nation's history, culture, and social fabric. They serve as a reminder of the island's vibrant and multifaceted identity, where linguistic diversity is celebrated as a source of strength and unity in this enchanting land.

# Religions and Spirituality in Sri Lanka

Sri Lanka, a land renowned for its cultural diversity and historical depth, is a place where religions and spirituality have played a central role in shaping the lives of its people for centuries. The island's religious landscape is a reflection of its multicultural heritage, where various faiths coexist and contribute to the nation's rich tapestry of beliefs and traditions.

Buddhism, one of the world's oldest religions, holds a predominant place in Sri Lanka. Introduced to the island in the 3rd century BCE, Buddhism has been a driving force behind the island's cultural and ethical values. The majority of Sri Lankans, particularly the Sinhalese population, identify as Buddhists. The ancient city of Anuradhapura, with its majestic stupas and monastic complexes, stands as a testament to the profound influence of Buddhism on the island's history and architecture.

Hinduism, the second-largest religion in Sri Lanka, is predominantly practiced by the Tamil community, particularly in the northern and eastern regions. The temples dedicated to various deities, including Lord Shiva, Lord Vishnu, and Goddess Kali, are significant spiritual landmarks. The grand Nallur Kandaswamy Kovil in Jaffna and the historic Koneswaram Temple in Trincomalee are iconic Hindu religious sites that bear witness to the enduring presence of Hinduism on the island.

Islam has a substantial following in Sri Lanka, primarily among the Muslim community, known as the Moors. Mosques dot the landscape, and Islamic traditions and festivals are an integral part of the island's cultural fabric. The Jami Ul-Alfar Mosque in Colombo, with its striking red and white brickwork, is an architectural marvel that exemplifies Islamic influence in Sri Lanka.

Christianity, introduced to Sri Lanka during colonial times, has a notable presence, with both Catholics and Protestants forming Christian communities. St. Anthony's Shrine in Kochchikade, Colombo, and St. Sebastian's Church in Negombo are among the many Christian places of worship that reflect the enduring Christian heritage on the island.

In addition to these major religions, Sri Lanka is also home to smaller religious communities, including Buddhists and Hindus of Burmese and Malay descent, as well as adherents of indigenous belief systems like animism and ancestor worship, particularly among the Vedda people.

The religious landscape of Sri Lanka is marked by a spirit of tolerance and coexistence. Interfaith dialogue and mutual respect are woven into the social fabric, despite historical and political challenges that have at times strained relations among communities.

Religion in Sri Lanka extends beyond worship to influence everyday life, from festivals and rituals to art, music, and cuisine. It serves as a moral compass and a source of solace for the island's people, providing guidance and comfort in times of joy and adversity.

The religions and spirituality in Sri Lanka collectively contribute to the nation's identity, values, and cultural richness. They are an integral part of the island's story, reflecting its resilience, diversity, and the enduring quest for meaning and transcendence in this captivating land.

# Traditional Festivals and Celebrations

Sri Lanka, a land steeped in culture and tradition, is a place where festivities and celebrations are an integral part of life. The island's calendar is dotted with a colorful tapestry of traditional festivals and cultural celebrations, each with its unique significance and rituals.

One of the most prominent and widely celebrated festivals in Sri Lanka is the Sinhala and Tamil New Year, known as "Aluth Avurudda" or "Puthandu." It usually falls in April and marks the beginning of the traditional farming season. Families come together to prepare special dishes, engage in customs like lighting the hearth, and partake in auspicious activities to welcome the New Year.

The Esala Perahera, or the Kandy Perahera, is a grand religious procession held annually in the city of Kandy, typically in July or August. It's a vibrant and mesmerizing spectacle that honors the sacred Tooth Relic of the Buddha, which is housed in the Temple of the Tooth. The procession features traditional dancers, drummers, and beautifully adorned elephants, creating a captivating display of Sri Lankan culture and spirituality.

Vesak, also known as Buddha Purnima, is a significant Buddhist festival celebrated in May. It commemorates the birth, enlightenment, and death of Lord Buddha. Devotees across the country visit temples to make offerings and light lanterns, creating a serene and illuminated atmosphere.

Deepavali, or Diwali, is celebrated by the Tamil Hindu community with great fervor. It's the festival of lights, symbolizing the victory of light over darkness and good over evil. Homes are decorated with oil lamps, colorful rangoli patterns adorn doorsteps, and sweets are exchanged among families and friends.

Thaipongal, another important Tamil festival, is dedicated to honoring the sun god and expressing gratitude for a bountiful harvest. Families gather to prepare a special dish called "Pongal" made from newly harvested rice, symbolizing prosperity and abundance.

The Navam Perahera, held in Colombo in February, is another grand procession that showcases traditional Sri Lankan culture and Buddhist heritage. It features a stunning display of decorated elephants, traditional dancers, and musicians parading through the streets.

Eid-ul-Fitr and Eid-ul-Adha are significant Islamic festivals celebrated by the Muslim community. Eid-ul-Fitr marks the end of Ramadan, the holy month of fasting, and is a time for communal prayers and feasting. Eid-ul-Adha, known as the "Festival of Sacrifice," commemorates the willingness of Prophet Ibrahim (Abraham) to sacrifice his son and is marked by the sacrifice of animals and acts of charity.

Christmas, celebrated by Christians, is a time of religious observance and festivity. Midnight Mass services are attended, and homes are adorned with Christmas decorations. In some areas, traditional Christmas sweets like "kokis" and "athirasa" are prepared.

Sri Lanka's cultural and religious diversity is beautifully reflected in its festivals and celebrations. These events not only provide an opportunity for communities to come together but also offer a glimpse into the island's rich heritage and the enduring spirit of its people. Whether it's lighting oil lamps, parading elephants, or sharing festive meals, these traditions form an integral part of Sri Lanka's cultural tapestry, creating memories and connections that span generations.

# Arts and Crafts of Sri Lanka

Sri Lanka's rich cultural heritage is beautifully expressed through its vibrant arts and crafts, which are a testament to the island's creativity, craftsmanship, and diverse traditions. From intricate handwoven textiles to intricately carved woodwork, the arts and crafts of Sri Lanka are a reflection of its history, culture, and the ingenuity of its people.

One of the most celebrated forms of traditional craftsmanship in Sri Lanka is handloom weaving. The country has a long history of producing exquisite textiles, with regions like Kandy, Kurunegala, and Ambalangoda known for their distinct weaving styles. Skilled artisans use manual looms to create an array of fabrics, including saris, sarongs, and traditional attire, known as "osariya." These textiles often feature intricate patterns and vibrant colors, making them highly sought after both locally and internationally.

Wood carving is another prominent craft in Sri Lanka, with a tradition that dates back centuries. Highly skilled woodcarvers create intricate designs on furniture, doors, and temple architecture. The city of Galle, with its Dutch-influenced architecture and ornate woodwork, is a testament to the island's woodcarving heritage.

Metalwork in Sri Lanka is marked by exceptional craftsmanship, particularly in the creation of brass and copper items. Skilled artisans produce decorative objects like lamps, vases, and jewelry boxes, often adorned with intricate filigree work and detailed engravings. These pieces showcase the meticulous attention to detail and artistic flair of

Sri Lankan metalworkers. Pottery and ceramics have a long history on the island, with distinctive styles emerging from different regions. The village of Matale, for example, is known for its traditional clay pottery, including unique cooking pots and utensils. Meanwhile, Batik, a method of dyeing fabric using wax-resistant techniques, is widely practiced in Sri Lanka. The Batik process results in intricate and colorful designs on textiles, and the town of Kandy is a notable center for Batik production.

Sri Lankan traditional masks are not just artistic creations but also a vital part of cultural performances and rituals. Craftsmen carve these masks with precision, each design representing a character from folklore or traditional drama. Masks are often used in rituals to invoke blessings or ward off evil spirits.

Basket weaving and pottery-making are also integral to Sri Lanka's traditional crafts, with local communities passing down these skills from generation to generation. Baskets, made from materials like cane and rattan, serve both practical and decorative purposes, while pottery is essential for cooking and storage. The island's artistic heritage is also reflected in its thriving contemporary art scene. Sri Lankan artists, both traditional and modern, have gained recognition on the global stage for their diverse and innovative works, exploring themes that range from spirituality to social issues.

In Sri Lanka, the arts and crafts are more than just expressions of creativity; they are a reflection of the nation's identity and cultural diversity. Each piece crafted by skilled hands carries with it a piece of history, tradition, and the enduring spirit of a people deeply connected to their heritage.

# Music and Dance of the Island

Sri Lanka's music and dance are a vibrant expression of the island's cultural diversity and deep-rooted traditions. These artistic forms have evolved over centuries, reflecting the nation's rich heritage, religious influences, and the rhythms of daily life.

Traditional Sri Lankan music is a harmonious blend of indigenous melodies and instruments, with influences from neighboring South Asian countries. The country's music is characterized by its intricate rhythms and melodic patterns, often played on traditional instruments such as the "geta bera" (a type of drum), "yak bera" (a smaller drum), and the "raban" (a hand-held drum). These instruments are central to religious and cultural ceremonies, and their rhythms are an integral part of traditional dances.

Dance, like music, holds a significant place in Sri Lankan culture, with various forms of dance practiced across the island. One of the most well-known traditional dances is "Kandyan dance," which originates from the central highlands around Kandy. Dancers in elaborate costumes, including headdresses adorned with peacock feathers, perform intricate footwork and expressive movements, often accompanied by drummers and flutists. Kandyan dance is frequently seen in religious and cultural festivals, captivating audiences with its dynamic energy.

The "Low Country dance" is another traditional dance form, primarily practiced in the coastal regions of Sri Lanka. Dancers, often in colorful attire, perform graceful movements and symbolic gestures that tell stories from folklore and mythology. The "Thovil" dance, associated with exorcism rituals, is another fascinating dance form in the low country. Sri Lanka's cultural tapestry also includes "Sabaragamuwa dance," originating from the Sabaragamuwa province. This dance form is characterized by its elegant and slow-paced movements, often depicting themes from the region's agricultural traditions and rituals.

Religious festivals play a vital role in showcasing Sri Lanka's music and dance. The annual "Esala Perahera" in Kandy is a grand procession that features not only the veneration of the sacred Tooth Relic but also a spectacular display of traditional music and dance. Drummers, flutists, and dancers clad in vibrant costumes take part in this magnificent cultural event. In addition to traditional forms, Sri Lanka has a burgeoning contemporary music scene. Modern genres such as pop, rock, and hip-hop have gained popularity among the island's youth, with Sri Lankan artists making their mark both nationally and internationally.

The fusion of traditional and contemporary elements is also evident in Sri Lankan music. Musicians often experiment with blending traditional instruments and melodies with modern beats, creating a unique and dynamic sound that appeals to a wide audience.

Sri Lanka's music and dance are more than just artistic expressions; they are a way of preserving and celebrating the island's rich cultural heritage. They connect generations, serve as a form of storytelling, and provide a means of connecting with the divine. Whether it's the rhythms of traditional drums or the graceful movements of dancers, Sri Lanka's music and dance continue to enchant and inspire, echoing the island's enduring spirit.

# Culinary Delights: Sri Lankan Cuisine

Sri Lankan cuisine is a flavorful and diverse reflection of the island's rich history, cultural influences, and natural bounty. With its aromatic spices, tropical ingredients, and a blend of culinary traditions, Sri Lankan food is a tantalizing journey for the senses.

Rice is the staple food of Sri Lanka and forms the foundation of almost every meal. It's typically served with an array of curries, each featuring a unique combination of spices and ingredients. Coconut, both in the form of coconut milk and grated coconut, is a common and essential component in Sri Lankan cooking, lending a rich and creamy texture to many dishes.

One of the signature dishes of Sri Lankan cuisine is "rice and curry." This consists of rice served with an assortment of curries, which can include meat, fish, or vegetables. These curries are prepared with a blend of spices, such as cardamom, cinnamon, cloves, and curry leaves, creating a symphony of flavors. "Sambol," a spicy condiment made with coconut, chili, and other ingredients, often accompanies rice and curry, adding an extra kick to the meal.

Seafood plays a prominent role in Sri Lankan cuisine, given the island's coastal location. Fish is prepared in various ways, from being curried with spices to being marinated in coconut milk and grilled. "Ambul Thiyal," a tangy and spicy fish curry, is a notable dish that originated in the southern region. Sri Lanka's vegetable curries are equally delightful, with ingredients like brinjal (eggplant), okra, and jackfruit taking center stage. "Gotu Kola Sambol," a salad made with finely chopped gotu kola leaves, coconut, and lime juice, is a refreshing side dish.

The island is also famous for its "hoppers," a type of bowl-shaped pancake made from fermented rice flour. Hoppers come in various forms, including "egg hoppers" with an egg cracked into the center, and "string hoppers," which are steamed rice noodles. Devotees of spice will find their palates satisfied in Sri Lanka. "Lunu miris," a fiery chili paste, is a popular accompaniment for those who enjoy the heat. "Pol sambol," a mixture of grated coconut, chili, and other spices, provides a milder yet flavorful alternative.

Sri Lanka's sweets and desserts are equally enticing. "Watalappan," a steamed coconut custard, and "kiri pani," a sweet milk pudding, are just a couple of the delectable options. "Kavum" and "kokis" are deep-fried sweets traditionally made during special occasions.

Tea is an integral part of Sri Lankan culture and economy. The country is renowned for its tea plantations, and "Ceylon tea" is celebrated globally for its quality and flavor. Visitors can explore tea estates in the hill country, where they can witness the tea-making process and enjoy a steaming cup of freshly brewed tea.

Sri Lankan cuisine is a harmonious blend of flavors, textures, and aromas. It reflects the island's culinary creativity and the warmth of its people who take pride in sharing their delightful dishes. From street food stalls to upscale restaurants, Sri Lankan cuisine offers a gastronomic adventure that is as diverse and vibrant as the island itself.

# Exotic Flavors and Ingredients

Sri Lankan cuisine is a vibrant tapestry of exotic flavors and ingredients that tantalize the taste buds and transport diners to a world of culinary delight. The island's unique geographical location, nestled in the Indian Ocean, has made it a treasure trove of diverse ingredients and spices that have shaped its distinct culinary identity.

Spices are at the heart of Sri Lankan cooking, and the country is often referred to as the "Spice Island." The use of spices like cardamom, cinnamon, cloves, and nutmeg infuses Sri Lankan dishes with depth and complexity. These spices are not only used for their flavor but also for their medicinal properties, making Sri Lankan cuisine a fusion of taste and wellness.

One of the most iconic spices in Sri Lankan cuisine is "Ceylon cinnamon." Known for its sweet and aromatic flavor, Ceylon cinnamon is considered the true cinnamon and is prized for its quality. It is used in a variety of dishes, from savory curries to sweet desserts, imparting a warm and inviting aroma.

"Curry leaves" are another essential ingredient in Sri Lankan cooking. These fragrant leaves are often used to add a citrusy and herbal note to curries, providing a distinctive flavor that is unique to the region. Combined with other spices, curry leaves create a harmonious balance of tastes in many Sri Lankan dishes.

Coconut, in its various forms, is a fundamental ingredient in Sri Lankan cuisine. "Coconut milk" is used to create creamy and luscious curries, while "grated coconut" adds texture and flavor to dishes like "pol sambol" and "kiri hodi." The versatility of coconut in Sri Lankan cooking is unparalleled.

Sri Lanka's tropical climate also gives rise to a bounty of fresh fruits, such as "mangoes," "pineapples," "bananas," and "papayas." These fruits are not only enjoyed as snacks but are also used to create refreshing fruit salads and chutneys that complement the spiciness of many Sri Lankan dishes.

"Jackfruit" is a unique and versatile ingredient in Sri Lankan cuisine. It can be used when unripe as a vegetable in curries or when ripe as a sweet fruit. "Wood apple," locally known as "beli," is used to make a tangy and refreshing drink called "wood apple juice."

Seafood is abundant in Sri Lanka, and the "fish" used in its cuisine is exceptionally fresh and flavorful. "Maldive fish," a dried and cured tuna, is a common ingredient in Sri Lankan cooking, adding a savory and umami-rich dimension to various dishes.

Rice, particularly "red rice" and "samba rice," is the backbone of Sri Lankan meals. These varieties of rice are aromatic and nutritious, serving as the perfect canvas for the rich and diverse flavors of curries and accompaniments.

"Gotu kola," a leafy green herb, is used in salads and sambols, adding a fresh and earthy flavor. "Dried chili" and "black pepper" are used to impart heat and spice to dishes, while "turmeric" provides a warm and golden hue to many Sri Lankan curries.

Sri Lankan cuisine's exotic flavors and ingredients are a testament to the island's culinary prowess and its ability to weave together diverse elements into a harmonious and delectable tapestry. Each bite is an exploration of taste, a journey into the heart of an ancient culture that continues to captivate the world with its gastronomic treasures.

# Sri Lankan Street Food

The bustling streets of Sri Lanka are a gastronomic paradise, where the aroma of sizzling spices and the siren call of street vendors create an irresistible tapestry of flavors. Sri Lankan street food is a vibrant and essential part of the island's culinary culture, offering a sensory journey that captures the heart and soul of this enchanting nation.

One of the most beloved street food items in Sri Lanka is the "kottu roti." This delectable dish features chopped flatbread stir-fried with an assortment of ingredients, including vegetables, eggs, and your choice of protein, typically chicken or beef. The whole concoction is seasoned with a blend of spices and sauces, resulting in a symphony of textures and flavors. The rhythmic clanging of the spatulas on the griddle as the kottu roti is prepared is a familiar sound on Sri Lankan streets.

"Isso wade," or prawn fritters, are another street food favorite. These crispy delights are made by mixing prawns with a spiced batter and frying them to perfection. Isso wade stalls often dot the coastal areas, where fresh seafood is abundant.

"Short eats" are savory snacks that can be found at nearly every street corner. These include "fish buns," "vegetable roti," and "egg rolls." These handheld treats are perfect for a quick and satisfying bite on the go.

"String hoppers" are often sold as a street food item, served with a variety of spicy sambols or curries. These delicate, steamed rice noodles are a staple in Sri Lankan cuisine and are a must-try for any visitor. For those seeking a spicy kick, "kottu roti" and "hoppers" often come with a side of "lunu miris," a fiery chili paste that adds an extra punch to your meal. Be warned; it can be incredibly hot!

If you're wandering the streets in the evening, you might come across " isso vadai" stalls. These are deep-fried lentil patties topped with succulent prawns, creating a satisfying and flavorful combination.

"Polos," or young jackfruit curry, is a vegetarian street food option that offers a unique taste experience. The jackfruit is cooked until tender and infused with a rich blend of spices, resulting in a delicious and meaty texture.

"Roti," a type of flatbread, is commonly sold by street vendors. These can be plain or stuffed with various fillings, such as "parippu" (dhal), "potato curry," or even "sambol." They are folded into neat parcels and make for a convenient and tasty snack.

Sri Lankan sweets also make their presence felt on the streets. "Kavum" and "kokis" are deep-fried sweets that are popular during festive seasons but can often be found at street stalls. "Aasmi" is another sweet treat made from rice flour and drizzled with sweet syrup.

Sri Lankan street food is a reflection of the island's diverse culinary heritage and a testament to its people's creativity and resourcefulness. Whether you're exploring the vibrant streets of Colombo, the coastal towns, or the bustling markets of Kandy, indulging in Sri Lankan street food is an adventure for the senses, offering an authentic taste of this captivating island nation.

# Wildlife Wonders of Sri Lanka

Sri Lanka, often referred to as the "Pearl of the Indian Ocean," is a land of astonishing natural beauty and biodiversity. Its rich tapestry of landscapes, from lush rainforests to arid plains, is home to an array of unique and diverse wildlife species, making it a paradise for nature enthusiasts and wildlife lovers.

One of Sri Lanka's most iconic and celebrated wildlife residents is the "Sri Lankan elephant." These majestic creatures roam the island's national parks and wildlife sanctuaries, and they are considered one of the country's cultural symbols. The Udawalawe and Minneriya National Parks are renowned for their large gatherings of elephants, known as "the Gathering," a truly mesmerizing spectacle.

Sri Lanka is also famous for its leopards. The elusive "Sri Lankan leopard" is a subspecies found only on the island, particularly in the Yala National Park. With its distinct spotted coat, the leopard is a top predator in Sri Lanka's ecosystem.

Birdwatchers are in for a treat in Sri Lanka, as the country boasts over 400 species of birds. The "Sri Lanka junglefowl" is the national bird and a common sight in the country's forests. Bird enthusiasts can spot vibrant species like the "Sri Lanka blue magpie" and the "Sri Lanka hanging parrot."

The island's tropical rainforests are home to a wealth of biodiversity. The "Sri Lankan purple-faced langur" is an endemic primate known for its distinctive purple face. Sri Lanka's forests are also inhabited by various species of squirrels, reptiles, and amphibians.

For those fascinated by marine life, Sri Lanka offers excellent opportunities for whale watching. The waters off the coast are home to numerous species of whales and dolphins, including the "blue whale," the largest animal on Earth. Mirissa, Dondra Point, and Trincomalee are popular whale-watching destinations.

Sri Lanka's coastal areas are teeming with marine biodiversity. Coral reefs thrive in the warm waters, offering a glimpse into the underwater world. Snorkeling and diving enthusiasts can explore vibrant coral gardens and encounter colorful fish, sea turtles, and even reef sharks.

The island's national parks and wildlife reserves provide sanctuaries for a wide range of animals. "Yala National Park" is not only known for its leopards but also for its diverse birdlife and populations of deer, wild boar, and crocodiles. "Wilpattu National Park" is another wildlife haven, where visitors can spot sloth bears, spotted deer, and a variety of avian species.

Sri Lanka's commitment to conservation is evident in its network of protected areas and its efforts to preserve endangered species. The "Sinharaja Forest Reserve," a UNESCO World Heritage Site, is a prime example of the island's dedication to safeguarding its unique biodiversity.

In Sri Lanka, the marvels of nature are never far away. The wildlife wonders of this island nation, with its lush landscapes and remarkable creatures, beckon travelers to explore and appreciate the awe-inspiring beauty of the natural world. Whether it's tracking elephants in the wild, spotting leopards, or observing marine life in the deep blue ocean, Sri Lanka's wildlife is a testament to the importance of conservation and the remarkable biodiversity that thrives on this captivating island.

# The Importance of Conservation

In the heart of the Indian Ocean lies an island nation that boasts an incredible array of biodiversity, and that nation is Sri Lanka. With its stunning landscapes, lush rainforests, and diverse ecosystems, Sri Lanka is a natural wonder. Yet, this natural beauty faces ongoing challenges, making the importance of conservation paramount in preserving the island's unique flora and fauna.

Sri Lanka is home to a remarkable range of wildlife, from the majestic elephants that roam its national parks to the elusive leopards that prowl its forests. The rich avian diversity, the unique primates like the purple-faced langur, and the marine life that thrives in its coastal waters all contribute to the island's natural wealth.

Conservation in Sri Lanka extends beyond safeguarding iconic species. It encompasses the protection of critical habitats such as rainforests, wetlands, and coral reefs. The "Sinharaja Forest Reserve," a UNESCO World Heritage Site, is one such example. This lush rainforest, often referred to as the "Lion Kingdom," is a sanctuary for countless species found nowhere else on Earth.

The coral reefs that fringe Sri Lanka's coastline are vital for both marine life and the communities that depend on them. Coral conservation efforts are essential to combat the effects of climate change and pollution, ensuring the long-term survival of these delicate ecosystems.

Conservation initiatives in Sri Lanka are not solely focused on preserving the environment but also on empowering local communities. Sustainable ecotourism provides livelihoods for many and fosters a sense of stewardship among those who live in close proximity to wildlife habitats. The "Human-Elephant Conflict" is a significant challenge in Sri Lanka. As human populations expand into traditional elephant territories, conflicts arise, posing a threat to both elephants and people. Conservation organizations work tirelessly to mitigate these conflicts through innovative strategies and community engagement.

Conservationists in Sri Lanka also recognize the importance of educating future generations about the value of their natural heritage. Environmental education programs and outreach efforts aim to instill a sense of responsibility for the environment in the youth of the nation.

The importance of conservation in Sri Lanka cannot be overstated. It's not just about protecting individual species or preserving picturesque landscapes; it's about maintaining the delicate balance of ecosystems, ensuring the well-being of communities, and securing a sustainable future for all.

The challenges faced by Sri Lanka's natural world are complex and multifaceted, from habitat loss and poaching to climate change and human-wildlife conflicts. However, the dedication of conservationists, the involvement of local communities, and the support of the global community provide hope for the island's future.

Sri Lanka's commitment to conservation serves as an example of what can be achieved when people come together to protect the environment. It's a testament to the enduring connection between humans and nature, a bond that must be preserved for generations to come. The importance of conservation in Sri Lanka is not just a chapter in its story; it's a legacy that will shape the nation's future and the fate of its incredible natural wonders.

# National Parks and Sanctuaries

Sri Lanka's natural treasures are safeguarded in a network of national parks and wildlife sanctuaries that span the island, each offering a unique glimpse into the country's incredible biodiversity. These protected areas play a vital role in preserving the island's rich natural heritage and ensuring the survival of its unique flora and fauna.

"Yala National Park," situated in the southeast of the island, is one of the most famous and visited national parks in Sri Lanka. It's renowned for its diverse wildlife, including the elusive Sri Lankan leopard, which prowls the park's dense jungles. Yala is also home to elephants, sloth bears, crocodiles, and numerous bird species. The park's landscape varies from coastal dunes to lush forests, making it a fascinating ecosystem to explore.

Udawalawe National Park, located in the southern part of Sri Lanka, is celebrated for its large population of elephants. The Udawalawe Reservoir, at the park's center, provides a vital water source for these gentle giants and other wildlife. Visitors to Udawalawe can witness herds of elephants up close and personal during safaris.

Minneriya National Park, in the North Central Province, is famous for hosting the annual "Gathering of Elephants." During the dry season, hundreds of elephants congregate around the Minneriya Tank in search of water and food. This natural spectacle is one of Sri Lanka's most remarkable wildlife events.

Wilpattu National Park, located in the northwest, is known for its unique landscape of "villus" (natural lakes) and pristine forests. The park is home to diverse wildlife, including leopards, sloth bears, spotted deer, and a variety of bird species. Wilpattu's untouched beauty and wilderness make it a haven for nature enthusiasts.

Sinharaja Forest Reserve, a UNESCO World Heritage Site in the southwest, is a lush tropical rainforest that's home to numerous endemic species. This primeval forest is teeming with biodiversity, from colorful birds like the Sri Lanka blue magpie to unique amphibians and reptiles. Sinharaja is a haven for researchers and those looking to explore pristine wilderness.

Horton Plains National Park, situated in the central highlands, offers a different landscape entirely. The park's rolling grasslands, cloud forests, and the famous "World's End" viewpoint provide a unique experience. Horton Plains is home to the elusive "sambar deer" and numerous bird species.

Sri Lanka's coastal areas are dotted with marine and bird sanctuaries. "Bundala National Park" is a vital wetland habitat for migratory birds, particularly during the winter months. The "Bar Reef Marine Sanctuary" off the northwest coast is a haven for coral and marine life.

These national parks and sanctuaries serve not only as vital habitats for wildlife but also as ecotourism destinations. Visitors have the opportunity to explore Sri Lanka's natural wonders, engage with local communities, and contribute to conservation efforts.

The protection and preservation of these national parks and sanctuaries are paramount to ensuring that future generations can continue to marvel at the wonders of Sri Lanka's natural world. These protected areas are not just chapters in the country's conservation story; they are the living, breathing heart of an island nation that cherishes its unique and irreplaceable biodiversity.

# Sri Lanka's Breathtaking Beaches

Nestled in the azure embrace of the Indian Ocean, Sri Lanka boasts some of the most breathtaking beaches in the world. With its golden sands, swaying palms, and crystal-clear waters, the coastline of this tropical island paradise is a haven for sun-seekers, surfers, and those in search of serenity.

The southwestern coast of Sri Lanka is dotted with a string of idyllic beaches that cater to every traveler's taste. "Unawatuna Beach," just a short drive from the historic city of Galle, is renowned for its calm and clear waters, making it an ideal spot for swimming and snorkeling. The picturesque crescent-shaped bay is framed by lush green hills, creating a postcard-worthy backdrop.

"Mirissa Beach," not far from Unawatuna, is a laid-back beach town known for its tranquil ambiance. It's also a popular starting point for whale watching excursions, allowing visitors to witness the majesty of the world's largest mammal in its natural habitat.

For surf enthusiasts, the southern coast offers some of the best waves in Asia. "Hikkaduwa Beach" is a surfing hotspot, attracting wave riders from around the globe. The vibrant beach town also offers a lively nightlife scene and an array of beachfront bars and restaurants.

Traveling east from Hikkaduwa, you'll encounter "Bentota Beach." This tranquil stretch of coastline is perfect for those seeking a relaxed beach experience. Bentota is also known for its water sports activities, including jet skiing and parasailing.

Further along the southern coast, "Tangalle Beach" offers a quieter and less touristy atmosphere. Here, you can stroll along deserted shores, enjoy the shade of swaying palm trees, and take in the unspoiled beauty of nature.

The southern coast is not the only region that showcases Sri Lanka's coastal splendor. The eastern coast, with its pristine and less-visited beaches, offers a more secluded escape. "Arugam Bay" is a mecca for surfers, known for its world-class waves and a laid-back, bohemian vibe.

"Trincomalee," located on the northeast coast, boasts some of the most beautiful beaches in Sri Lanka. "Nilaveli Beach" and "Uppuveli Beach" are famous for their powdery white sands and clear blue waters. Trincomalee is also a gateway to diving adventures in the surrounding coral reefs.

The northern coast of Sri Lanka, which was once less accessible due to conflict, is now opening up to tourists, revealing pristine beaches that have remained untouched for decades. "Jaffna Peninsula" and "Mannar Island" are emerging as destinations for those seeking unspoiled coastal beauty.

The island's western coast, near the capital city of Colombo, offers its own share of charming beaches. "Mount Lavinia Beach" is a favorite weekend retreat for city dwellers, offering a blend of urban convenience and seaside relaxation.

Sri Lanka's coastline is not only a place of natural beauty but also a testament to the island's rich cultural heritage. Coastal towns and fishing villages offer a glimpse into traditional Sri Lankan life, with vibrant markets, colorful fishing boats, and friendly locals.

From vibrant surf towns to tranquil coves, Sri Lanka's beaches are a testament to the island's diversity and natural beauty. Whether you're seeking adventure, relaxation, or a taste of local culture, the pristine shores of Sri Lanka invite you to experience the magic of its breathtaking beaches, where the sunsets are unforgettable, the waves are inviting, and the sands are waiting to embrace your footsteps.

# Enchanting Hill Country and Tea Plantations

As you journey inland from Sri Lanka's coastal splendor, you'll find yourself enveloped in the enchanting embrace of the Hill Country, a region that beckons with its cool climate, lush green landscapes, and endless expanses of emerald tea plantations. This is a world apart, where the air is crisp, the vistas are breathtaking, and the scent of tea leaves wafts on the breeze.

The Hill Country is a haven for nature lovers and those seeking respite from the tropical heat. At the heart of this region lies "Nuwara Eliya," often referred to as "Little England." Its colonial architecture, including red-brick buildings and manicured gardens, harks back to the days when British tea planters sought refuge in this idyllic setting. The town's cool climate earned it the nickname "City of Eternal Spring."

Venture further into the hills, and you'll discover "Ella," a small town nestled amidst stunning landscapes. Ella is renowned for its dramatic views, particularly from the summit of "Ella Rock" and "Little Adam's Peak." These vantage points offer panoramic vistas of rolling hills, deep valleys, and cascading waterfalls, creating an otherworldly tableau.

The crown jewel of Sri Lanka's Hill Country is its vast tea plantations, which drape the hills like a verdant tapestry. The British introduced tea cultivation to Sri Lanka in the 19th century, and today, the country is one of the world's largest tea producers. "Ceylon Tea" is famous for its quality and flavor, and you can visit the plantations to witness the meticulous process of tea production. "Haputale," another charming hill town, offers a quieter and less touristy experience. Here, you can embark on picturesque hikes through tea gardens and explore the legendary "Lipton's Seat," a viewpoint that offers a glimpse into the legacy of Sir Thomas Lipton, one of the pioneers of Ceylon tea.

Sri Lanka's Hill Country is also home to several national parks and nature reserves, each with its own unique charm. "Horton Plains National Park" features rolling grasslands, cloud forests, and the iconic "World's End" viewpoint, where you can gaze out over a sheer precipice into the lush valleys below.

The Hill Country's stunning landscapes are also adorned with picturesque waterfalls. "Ramboda Falls," "Diyaluma Falls," and "Bambarakanda Falls" are among the most captivating, offering opportunities for hiking, photography, or simply taking in the natural beauty.

The region's cooler climate is ideal for growing a variety of fruits and vegetables. "Strawberries" thrive in the cool temperatures of Nuwara Eliya, and you can pick your own berries at local farms. The Hill Country is also known for its delicious "avocado" and "mandarin orange" varieties.

The journey through Sri Lanka's Hill Country is a sensory experience, where the gentle rolling hills, the symphony of birdcalls, and the aroma of fresh tea leaves combine to create an atmosphere of tranquility and wonder. It's a place where time seems to slow down, inviting you to savor the beauty of the moment and immerse yourself in the enchantment of the Hill Country and its tea plantations.

# Ancient Cities and Historical Sites

Sri Lanka is a treasure trove of history and ancient civilization, a place where the echoes of centuries past can still be heard in the whispers of ancient cities and the towering monuments that have withstood the test of time. From the ruins of regal kingdoms to sacred temples that have witnessed the ebb and flow of dynasties, the historical sites of Sri Lanka offer a journey through time like no other.

"Anuradhapura," one of the oldest continuously inhabited cities in the world, was the capital of ancient Sri Lanka for over a thousand years. This sprawling archaeological site is home to an array of monumental stupas, intricate carvings, and sacred bodhi trees. The "Sri Maha Bodhi," a sacred fig tree believed to have grown from a cutting of the original tree under which Buddha attained enlightenment, is a spiritual centerpiece of the city.

"Polonnaruwa," another ancient capital, showcases the remarkable achievements of Sri Lanka's past rulers. The "Royal Palace," "Gal Vihara" with its colossal stone Buddha statues, and the "Parakrama Samudraya" tank, a marvel of ancient irrigation, are testament to the grandeur of this bygone era.

"Sigiriya," often referred to as the "Lion Rock," is an iconic UNESCO World Heritage Site. This colossal rock fortress, adorned with frescoes and terraced gardens, was once the palace of King Kasyapa. Climbing to the summit provides not only breathtaking views but also a glimpse into the architectural and engineering prowess of the time.

"Dambulla Cave Temple" is another wonder that time has preserved. This complex of cave temples, adorned with intricate murals and hundreds of Buddha statues, offers a glimpse into the spiritual devotion and artistic excellence of ancient Sri Lanka.

"Kandy," nestled amidst lush hills, is home to the "Temple of the Sacred Tooth Relic," one of the most revered religious sites in Sri Lanka. It houses a relic believed to be a tooth of Buddha and attracts pilgrims and visitors alike. The city's "Royal Palace" and "Peradeniya Botanical Gardens" are also reminders of its regal history.

The "Galle Fort," a UNESCO World Heritage Site, stands as a testament to Sri Lanka's colonial history. Built by the Portuguese in the 16th century and later fortified by the Dutch, it is a living museum of colonial architecture and a picturesque enclave along the southwestern coast.

"Sri Lanka's Cultural Triangle" is an area encompassing Anuradhapura, Polonnaruwa, and Sigiriya, where the vestiges of ancient civilization and culture converge. Exploring this region offers a comprehensive view of the island's historical richness.

Sri Lanka's history is not confined to grand monuments alone. The island is also dotted with "stupas," "vihara," and "dagobas," each with its own story to tell. The "Ruwanwelisaya Stupa" in Anuradhapura, the "Jetavanaramaya Stupa" in Polonnaruwa, and the "Ridi Vihara" in Kurunegala are just a few examples of these sacred structures.

These ancient cities and historical sites are more than just relics of the past; they are living testaments to the enduring spirit of a nation that has weathered centuries of change. They invite travelers to step back in time, to marvel at the ingenuity of ancient engineers, to contemplate the teachings of Buddha, and to witness the artistic achievements of a bygone era. Sri Lanka's historical sites are not mere chapters in a book; they are the pages that tell the story of a civilization, etched in stone and steeped in the sands of time.

# Kandy: The Cultural Heart of Sri Lanka

Nestled amidst the emerald hills of central Sri Lanka, Kandy stands as a testament to the island's rich cultural heritage and spiritual significance. As the last capital of the ancient Kings' era, this city holds a unique place in the hearts of Sri Lankans and all who visit. It's often described as the cultural heart of Sri Lanka, and a journey to this enchanting city is a journey into the very soul of the nation.

At the heart of Kandy lies the revered "Temple of the Sacred Tooth Relic," locally known as the "Dalada Maligawa." This temple houses a relic believed to be the tooth of Lord Buddha, making it one of the holiest shrines in Buddhism. The relic is enshrined within a golden casket, and its veneration has been a central aspect of Sri Lankan culture and religion for centuries.

The "Esala Perahera," an annual procession that takes place in Kandy, is one of the most spectacular and significant religious events in the country. During this grand festival, the sacred tooth relic is paraded through the streets in a magnificent procession featuring beautifully adorned elephants, traditional dancers, and fire-breathers. The Esala Perahera is a mesmerizing display of Sri Lankan culture and spirituality, drawing thousands of pilgrims and tourists alike. The city's colonial past is also evident in its architecture. The "Royal Palace of Kandy" stands as an architectural marvel, and its audience hall, "Magul Maduwa," is adorned with intricate carvings and beautiful wooden pillars. The "Peradeniya Botanical Gardens," once a royal pleasure garden, showcases a stunning collection of orchids, palms, and exotic plants, creating a serene oasis. Kandy's picturesque setting amidst lush hills adds to its charm. The "Kandy Lake," built by King Sri Wickrama Rajasinghe in the early 19th century, is a tranquil spot for a leisurely stroll, and its surroundings are a haven for birdwatchers.

The city's cultural vibrancy extends beyond its historic sites. Kandy is renowned for its traditional dance performances, where skilled dancers in elaborate costumes perform age-old rituals and storytelling through dance. These performances provide a glimpse into the island's rich folklore and mythology.

Kandy's central location in the island's hill country makes it an ideal base for exploring the surrounding regions. From here, you can venture to the tea plantations of Nuwara Eliya, visit the dramatic landscapes of Ella, or embark on hikes to the nearby Knuckles Mountain Range, a UNESCO World Heritage Site.

The bustling streets of Kandy offer a fusion of old and new, where local markets showcase colorful textiles, spices, and handicrafts. Traditional street food stalls and restaurants serve up delicious Sri Lankan cuisine, offering a tantalizing array of flavors for adventurous eaters.

Kandy, the cultural heart of Sri Lanka, is a city that resonates with history, spirituality, and artistic expression. It's a place where tradition and modernity coexist, where the past is honored, and the present is alive with the vibrancy of a living culture. A visit to Kandy is an immersive experience in the soul of Sri Lanka, where the echoes of centuries past continue to resonate in its temples, palaces, and the hearts of its people.

# Galle: A Living Fort

Nestled along the southwestern coast of Sri Lanka, Galle stands as a living testament to the island's colonial past and its remarkable ability to preserve history while embracing modernity. This coastal city is renowned for its well-preserved 17th-century fort, a UNESCO World Heritage Site, and it's a place where history, culture, and commerce converge in a vibrant and picturesque setting.

The "Galle Fort," also known as the "Dutch Fort" due to its origins as a Dutch colonial stronghold, is a masterpiece of fortification and urban planning. Its imposing ramparts, sturdy bastions, and cobbled streets evoke the bygone era of European colonialism in Sri Lanka. However, what makes Galle truly unique is that it is not just a historical relic but a thriving community where people live, work, and play amidst the fort's historic walls.

Wandering through the narrow streets of the Galle Fort, you'll encounter a rich tapestry of architectural styles and influences. Dutch colonial buildings with their distinctive gables coexist with British-era residences and Portuguese-influenced structures. The "Groote Kerk," a Dutch Reformed Church dating back to the 18th century, stands as a testament to the city's religious heritage.

Galle Fort is not just about architecture; it's a living museum of culture and art. The fort is home to a thriving community of artists, writers, and artisans who have transformed historic buildings into galleries, boutiques, and cafes. Strolling through these vibrant spaces, you can appreciate the fusion of tradition and contemporary creativity.

One of the iconic landmarks within the fort is the "Galle Lighthouse." Originally built by the British in 1939, this lighthouse is still operational, guiding ships safely into the harbor. It's a reminder of Galle's maritime importance and its enduring connection to the sea.

Galle's coastal setting adds to its charm. The fort is flanked by the Indian Ocean, and its ramparts offer spectacular views of the sea and the bustling harbor. The "Flag Rock Bastion," known as "Kala Bokka" in Sinhala, is a popular spot to catch mesmerizing sunsets and watch daring locals jump into the sea.

Galle's history isn't just confined to the fort itself; it extends to the nearby areas. The "Galle International Stadium," located just outside the fort, is a cricket ground with a rich history, hosting international matches amidst a backdrop of colonial-era buildings.

The "Galle Literary Festival" is an annual event that brings together renowned authors and literary enthusiasts from around the world. Held within the fort's historic venues, this festival celebrates literature, art, and culture.

Galle's vibrant streets come alive with markets selling everything from fresh produce to intricate handicrafts. The "Galle Fort Market" is a hub for artisanal products, offering a glimpse into the island's creative talents.

Galle is a city where history continues to be written, where the past and present coexist in harmony. It's a place where you can savor freshly caught seafood at a centuries-old restaurant, admire contemporary art in a Dutch-era warehouse, and witness the ongoing evolution of a living fort.

The essence of Galle lies not just in its stone walls but in the spirit of its people who have embraced the fort's rich heritage and transformed it into a thriving, dynamic community. Galle is more than a historical relic; it's a living, breathing testament to the enduring allure of Sri Lanka's coastal cities.

# Colombo: Sri Lanka's Bustling Capital

Nestled on the western coast of Sri Lanka, Colombo is the vibrant beating heart of the nation. As the capital and largest city, it's a bustling metropolis that encapsulates the island's diverse culture, rich history, and dynamic modernity. With a history dating back centuries and a contemporary spirit that's ever-evolving, Colombo is a city of contrasts and endless surprises.

The origins of Colombo can be traced back to ancient times when it was a trading hub for Arab, Persian, and Chinese merchants. Its strategic location along the historic Silk Road maritime route made it a coveted port for traders from around the world. Over the centuries, it has been ruled by various empires, including the Portuguese, Dutch, and British, each leaving their indelible mark on the city's culture and architecture.

Today, Colombo is a reflection of Sri Lanka's diversity. Its streets are a tapestry of languages, with Sinhala, Tamil, and English spoken in various corners of the city. This linguistic diversity mirrors the island's multicultural population, with Sinhalese, Tamil, Muslim, and Burgher communities coexisting harmoniously.

The heart of Colombo is "Galle Face Green," a sprawling seaside promenade that offers stunning views of the Indian Ocean. Here, you can witness breathtaking sunsets, savor street food delicacies, and enjoy a leisurely stroll along the waterfront. It's a gathering place for both locals and visitors, where the city's pulse can be felt.

Colombo's skyline is a blend of historic and modern architecture. The "Old Parliament Building" stands as a symbol of colonial heritage, while modern skyscrapers like the "Lotus Tower" showcase the city's contemporary ambitions. The "Independence Memorial Hall" is an architectural gem that commemorates Sri Lanka's independence from British rule.

"Colombo National Museum" is a treasure trove of historical artifacts, offering a glimpse into the island's past. Its collection includes ancient sculptures, traditional masks, and royal regalia. Nearby, the "Viharamahadevi Park" provides a green oasis in the heart of the city, perfect for a tranquil escape.

Colombo's markets are a sensory delight. "Pettah Market" is a bustling maze of narrow streets where you can shop for spices, textiles, and a myriad of goods. "Manning Market" is a vibrant place to experience the daily life of Colombo's fruit and vegetable traders. The "Good Market" offers a selection of organic and eco-friendly products.

The city's culinary scene is a reflection of its cosmopolitan nature. From traditional Sri Lankan rice and curry to international cuisine, Colombo offers a diverse range of dining experiences. "Street food" stalls serve up mouthwatering snacks like "kottu roti" and "isso vade," showcasing the island's flavors.

Colombo's nightlife is also thriving, with a range of bars, clubs, and live music venues. "Cinnamon Gardens" is a trendy neighborhood known for its upscale dining and entertainment options.

Colombo is not just a modern city; it's a hub for culture and the arts. The "Nelum Pokuna Mahinda Rajapaksa Theatre" hosts performances ranging from classical music to contemporary theater. The "Jana Kala Kendraya" is an art center promoting Sri Lankan visual and performing arts.

The city's religious diversity is evident in its numerous temples, churches, and mosques. The "Gangaramaya Temple" is a prominent Buddhist temple that also houses a museum. The "St. Anthony's Shrine" is a revered Catholic church, while the "Jami Ul-Alfar Mosque" is an architectural masterpiece.

Colombo's allure lies in its ability to blend the past with the present, the traditional with the contemporary. It's a city where ancient temples stand beside modern malls, where historic markets bustle with energy, and where the flavors of Sri Lanka mingle with international cuisines. Colombo is more than just a capital city; it's a vibrant reflection of Sri Lanka's diverse and ever-evolving identity.

# Jaffna: A Northern Gem

In the northern reaches of Sri Lanka lies a region that holds a unique place in the tapestry of the island's culture and history. Jaffna, often referred to as the "Cultural Capital of the North," is a land of resilience, rich traditions, and a distinct identity that has weathered the trials of time and conflict.

Jaffna's history stretches back millennia, with archaeological evidence suggesting human settlements dating as far back as the 2nd century BC. The city was a bustling center of trade and culture, connecting Sri Lanka to other parts of Asia and the Middle East. Its strategic location along ancient maritime routes made it a melting pot of cultures, with influences from India, the Arabian Peninsula, and beyond.

The Jaffna Peninsula is dotted with "kovils" or Hindu temples, reflecting the predominant religious and cultural influence in the region. The "Nallur Kandaswamy Kovil" is one of the most iconic, known for its vibrant festivals and intricate architecture. The annual "Nallur Festival" is a spectacle of music, dance, and devotion that draws pilgrims from across the island.

Jaffna's cultural richness extends to its cuisine, which is distinct from the rest of Sri Lanka. "Jaffna cuisine" is characterized by its use of fragrant spices, seafood, and unique dishes like "Jaffna crab curry" and "Jaffna mango curry." The city's markets are a feast for the senses, with vendors selling an array of fresh produce, spices, and traditional snacks. The Jaffna Peninsula is also home to pristine beaches like "Casuarina Beach" and "Chundikulam Beach," where turquoise waters meet sandy shores, offering a tranquil escape from the city's hustle and bustle. The "Jaffna Lagoon" is a thriving ecosystem and a haven for birdwatchers. During the Sri Lankan Civil War, Jaffna bore witness to its share of conflict and hardship. However, in the post-war era, the region has made significant strides in rebuilding and rejuvenating its cultural heritage. Efforts to restore historic sites and foster tourism have breathed new life into Jaffna.

The "Jaffna Public Library," once one of Asia's finest, was tragically destroyed during the conflict but has since been rebuilt as a symbol of cultural revival. Its shelves are now stocked with a wealth of literature, preserving knowledge and culture for future generations.

The "Jaffna Fort," with its iconic star-shaped design, is a testament to the city's colonial history. Built by the Portuguese in the 17th century and later expanded by the Dutch, the fort has witnessed centuries of change and transformation.

Jaffna's northernmost point, "Point Pedro," offers panoramic views of the Palk Strait and is a place of serene beauty. The "Keerimalai Springs," known for their healing properties, are a place of pilgrimage and tranquility.

The resilience and determination of Jaffna's people shine through in their efforts to preserve and celebrate their cultural heritage. The region is a living testament to the enduring spirit of Sri Lanka's northern gem, where history, culture, and tradition continue to flourish amidst the challenges of the past and the promise of the future.

# Anuradhapura: Sacred City and UNESCO World Heritage Site

In the heart of Sri Lanka's Northern Central Province lies the ancient city of Anuradhapura, a place of profound historical and spiritual significance. As one of the oldest continuously inhabited cities in the world, Anuradhapura boasts a rich heritage that spans over two millennia, earning it recognition as a UNESCO World Heritage Site. It is a city that resonates with the echoes of the past and stands as a testament to the island's enduring Buddhist traditions.

Anuradhapura served as the capital of Sri Lanka for over a thousand years, beginning in the 4th century BC when it was founded by King Pandukabhaya. This period marked the establishment of Buddhism in the country, and Anuradhapura became a center of religious and cultural growth. The city's significance was further cemented when it became home to the sacred "Sri Maha Bodhi," a sacred fig tree believed to have grown from a cutting of the original tree under which Buddha attained enlightenment in India.

The Sri Maha Bodhi is a revered symbol of Buddhism in Sri Lanka and is considered the oldest living human-planted tree in the world. Pilgrims from across the island and Buddhist devotees from around the globe visit Anuradhapura to pay their respects to this sacred tree, which continues to thrive in the "Mahavihara" complex.

One of the most iconic and enduring symbols of Anuradhapura is the "Ruwanwelisaya Stupa." Standing at an impressive 103 meters in height, it is one of the tallest stupas in Sri Lanka. This stupa, constructed by King Dutugemunu in the 2nd century BC, is a testament to the architectural and engineering prowess of ancient Sri Lankan civilization.

The "Jetavanaramaya Stupa" is another monumental structure that captures the imagination of visitors. It is believed to have been the largest stupa in the ancient world, surpassing even the dimensions of the Great Pyramids of Egypt. Its construction was a remarkable feat of engineering and craftsmanship.

Anuradhapura is also home to numerous other stupas, ancient monasteries, and intricate stone carvings that provide a glimpse into the artistic and spiritual achievements of the past. The "Abhayagiri Monastery" and the "Thuparamaya Stupa" are among the notable sites that showcase the city's historical and religious significance.

The city's complex irrigation systems, such as the "Jaya Sri Maha Bodhi Tank" and the "Tissa Wewa," are a testament to the advanced engineering knowledge of its ancient inhabitants. These reservoirs played a crucial role in sustaining the city's agriculture and livelihood.

While Anuradhapura's grandeur and significance are steeped in the past, it remains a living city. Devotees continue to visit its sacred sites, and the city is home to a thriving community. The "Isurumuniya Temple" is a living example, where daily rituals and worship continue amidst the ancient carvings.

Anuradhapura's history, preserved in its temples, stupas, and monastic complexes, offers a profound connection to the roots of Buddhism in Sri Lanka. It is a place where the spiritual and historical dimensions of the island converge, creating an enduring legacy that continues to inspire awe and reverence. As a UNESCO World Heritage Site, Anuradhapura invites travelers to step back in time, to marvel at the achievements of an ancient civilization, and to connect with the enduring spiritual traditions of Sri Lanka.

# Polonnaruwa: The Medieval Capital

Nestled in the heart of Sri Lanka, Polonnaruwa stands as a testament to the island's rich history and the enduring legacy of its medieval past. This ancient city, known as the second capital of Sri Lanka, offers a glimpse into a bygone era of grandeur, innovation, and cultural flourishing.

Polonnaruwa rose to prominence in the 11th century when King Vijayabahu I established it as the capital of the country, shifting the political center from the earlier capital, Anuradhapura. The move was prompted by invasions and the desire for a more defensible location, and it marked the beginning of Polonnaruwa's golden age.

The city's layout is a marvel of urban planning, with well-organized streets, reservoirs, and a complex irrigation system that supported a thriving agricultural economy. The "Parakrama Samudra," an immense reservoir built by King Parakramabahu I, is a testament to the advanced hydraulic engineering of the time. This vast reservoir, spread over an impressive 2,500 acres, not only served as a source of irrigation but also symbolized the power and vision of the rulers.

The "Royal Palace" complex, nestled in the heart of Polonnaruwa, showcases the architectural sophistication of the era. Though now mostly in ruins, it was once a grand palace adorned with intricate carvings and adorned with exotic wood. Adjacent to the palace stands the "Council Chamber," where the king would convene with his ministers to govern the kingdom. Polonnaruwa is renowned for its religious sites, which include some of the most exquisite examples of Sri Lankan art and architecture. The "Gal Vihara" or "Rock Temple" is home to four colossal Buddha statues carved into the granite rock, each exuding serenity and grace. The "Lankatilaka Temple" boasts a towering image of the Buddha, and the "Tivanka Image House" showcases vivid murals that depict scenes from the Buddha's life.

The "Rankot Vihara Stupa," one of the city's most iconic landmarks, is a towering brick monument that stands as a testament to the architectural prowess of the time. It is the largest stupa in Polonnaruwa and offers panoramic views of the cityscape.

Polonnaruwa's religious diversity is evident in its temples, including Hindu shrines like the "Hindu Kovil" and the "Siva Devalaya." These temples highlight the coexistence of different religious traditions during this era.

The "Potgul Vihara" is a unique structure that served as an audacious monastery for meditation. Its distinctive feature is a circular platform where monks practiced walking meditation, reflecting the contemplative spirit of the time.

The city's historical significance is further enhanced by the "Vatadage," an intricately carved circular relic house that once enshrined the sacred tooth relic of the Buddha. Its elegant stone carvings and guardstones are a testament to the craftsmanship of the era.

While Polonnaruwa's glory days are long past, the city's ruins offer a glimpse into a medieval world marked by artistic innovation, hydraulic engineering marvels, and profound spiritual devotion. It is a place where history comes to life, where the echoes of a bygone era resonate in the stone carvings and the tranquil waters of its reservoirs. Polonnaruwa, the medieval capital of Sri Lanka, is a living testament to the enduring legacy of a once-mighty kingdom.

# Sigiriya: The Rock Fortress

Amidst the lush greenery of Sri Lanka's central plains stands Sigiriya, an architectural marvel and UNESCO World Heritage Site that beckons travelers from across the globe. Often referred to as the "Eighth Wonder of the World," Sigiriya is a rock fortress that encapsulates the ingenuity, artistry, and historical significance of ancient Sri Lankan civilization.

The story of Sigiriya dates back to the 5th century AD, during the reign of King Kasyapa. Seeking to establish his capital on a grand scale, the king chose the towering monolith of Sigiriya as the foundation for his vision. What followed was a remarkable feat of engineering and artistry that transformed the rocky outcrop into a fortress and palace complex of unparalleled splendor.

One of the most iconic features of Sigiriya is the "Lion Rock," so named for the massive lion's paws that once flanked the entrance to the palace at the summit. These enormous stone paws, now the only remnants of the lion, stood as both a guard and a symbol of the king's might.

To ascend the rock, a complex system of stairways and walkways was constructed, with beautifully landscaped gardens, pools, and terraces along the way. The "Mirror Wall," a polished stone surface that retains its reflective quality to this day, is adorned with ancient graffiti and verses of admiration for the palace.

The "Frescoes of Sigiriya" are another remarkable aspect of this fortress. These vividly colored paintings, found on a sheltered rock face, depict a bevy of celestial maidens. Their graceful forms and intricate details offer a glimpse into the artistry of the time.

At the summit of Sigiriya lies the "Sigiriya Palace," a structure that once held the royal court and served as King Kasyapa's residence. The palace boasted a complex network of chambers, cisterns, and terraces, showcasing an advanced understanding of architecture and design. The panoramic views from the summit are awe-inspiring, offering a sweeping vista of the surrounding countryside.

The design of Sigiriya incorporated hydraulic engineering with advanced rainwater harvesting systems. The "Sigiriya Water Gardens" are a series of terraced pools, fountains, and conduits that demonstrate the intricate water management technology of the time.

The rock fortress of Sigiriya is not only a testament to the architectural and engineering prowess of its builders but also a reflection of their artistic sensibilities. It is a place where nature and human creativity harmoniously converge, creating an awe-inspiring testament to Sri Lanka's historical heritage.

Today, Sigiriya stands as a testament to the enduring legacy of ancient Sri Lankan civilization. It is a place where history, art, and nature intertwine, offering visitors a glimpse into the vision and ambition of King Kasyapa and the brilliance of the craftsmen and artists who brought his dream to life. Sigiriya remains a symbol of pride for Sri Lanka, a rock fortress that defies time and continues to inspire wonder and admiration.

# Dambulla: Cave Temples and Frescoes

Nestled in the heart of Sri Lanka's cultural triangle, the town of Dambulla is home to one of the country's most significant and awe-inspiring cultural treasures—the Dambulla Cave Temples. These ancient cave complexes, perched atop a massive granite outcrop, offer visitors a glimpse into the island's rich history, artistry, and spiritual heritage.

The Dambulla Cave Temples, also known as the "Golden Temple of Dambulla," are a complex of five cave temples that have been hewn out of the rock. Their origins date back to the 1st century BC when King Valagamba sought refuge in these caves during a period of exile. Following his return to the throne, he transformed these caves into a sacred sanctuary, a tradition that continued under successive rulers.

As you approach the caves, the sight of a massive golden Buddha statue, glistening in the sunlight, welcomes you. This colossal figure, known as the "Dambulla Cave Golden Buddha," stands as a symbol of the profound religious significance of the site.

Upon entering the caves, you are greeted by a breathtaking sight—a vast expanse of cave ceilings adorned with intricate and vibrant frescoes. These ancient paintings, which have stood the test of time for over two millennia, depict various scenes from the life of the Buddha and other religious narratives. The colors are still vivid, and the artistry remains a testament to the skill of the artists of yesteryears. The caves are divided into separate sections, each containing a wealth of religious statues, sculptures, and paintings. The "Devaraja Lena" or "Cave of the Divine King" houses an impressive reclining Buddha statue, while the "Maharaja Lena" or "Cave of the Great Kings" is adorned with a striking standing Buddha statue and numerous carvings.

The "Maha Alut Viharaya" or "Great New Temple" is a testament to the ongoing spiritual importance of Dambulla. Here, a magnificent seated Buddha statue takes center stage, surrounded by an array of smaller statues and offerings from devotees.

In addition to the religious significance, the Dambulla Cave Temples offer a captivating view of the surrounding countryside. Perched high on the rock, they provide a vantage point from which you can take in the picturesque landscapes of Sri Lanka's interior.

The Dambulla Cave Temples have been recognized as a UNESCO World Heritage Site, underscoring their cultural and historical significance. They continue to be a place of worship and pilgrimage, drawing both devout Buddhists and curious travelers who seek to connect with the island's spiritual and artistic heritage.

Dambulla, with its cave temples and frescoes, is a living testament to the enduring influence of Buddhism in Sri Lanka and the remarkable artistic achievements of its ancient civilization. It is a place where time stands still, and the echoes of devotion and creativity continue to reverberate through the centuries.

# The Spiritual Hub: Temple of the Tooth Relic

At the heart of Kandy, the cultural capital of Sri Lanka, lies the revered Temple of the Tooth Relic, known locally as "Sri Dalada Maligawa." This sacred site stands as a testament to the island's deep-rooted Buddhist heritage and houses one of the most venerated relics in the world—the tooth of Lord Buddha.

The history of the Temple of the Tooth Relic is intertwined with the history of Sri Lanka itself. It all began in the 4th century BC when the sacred tooth relic was brought to the island, concealed within the hair of Princess Hemamala, who fled India to protect the relic from hostile forces. The relic eventually found its way to the royal capital of Anuradhapura, where it was enshrined with great reverence.

Over the centuries, the tooth relic became a symbol of royal power and legitimacy. It was believed that possessing the relic conferred divine favor upon the reigning monarch. As a result, it was moved from capital to capital as the seat of power shifted within the island.

In the 16th century, during the reign of King Vimaladharmasuriya I, the tooth relic found its permanent home in Kandy, where a magnificent temple was built to house it. The Temple of the Tooth Relic, as it stands today, is a testament to the enduring devotion of the people of Sri Lanka.

The temple complex is a harmonious blend of architectural beauty and spiritual significance. As you approach the temple, you are greeted by a magnificent entrance, flanked by elephant statues, which symbolize the cultural importance of these majestic animals in Sri Lanka.

Inside the temple, the atmosphere is one of profound serenity and reverence. The central chamber, known as the "Pattirippuwa" or "Octagonal Pavilion," is where the tooth relic is enshrined. Visitors can catch a glimpse of the golden casket that contains the relic, although the casket is rarely opened for public viewing.

The temple is not only a place of worship but also a repository of priceless religious and cultural treasures. Its walls are adorned with intricate Kandyan art, and its halls house a remarkable collection of gifts and offerings from devotees and foreign dignitaries over the centuries.

One of the most captivating aspects of the Temple of the Tooth Relic is the daily rituals and ceremonies that take place. The "Pujas" or offerings are conducted with great pomp and pageantry, accompanied by traditional music and drumming. The annual "Esala Perahera" or the Festival of the Tooth, held in Kandy, is a grand procession that pays homage to the relic and showcases Sri Lanka's rich cultural heritage.

The Temple of the Tooth Relic is not merely a religious site; it is a living testament to the enduring faith and devotion of the Sri Lankan people. It stands as a symbol of unity and cultural pride, drawing pilgrims and tourists from around the world who seek to witness the spiritual heartbeat of the island.

As you stand in the presence of the sacred tooth relic, you can't help but be moved by the depth of faith and the centuries of history that it represents. The Temple of the Tooth Relic is not just a building; it is a living testament to the enduring power of spirituality and the cultural richness of Sri Lanka.

# Sri Lankan Traditional Medicine and Ayurveda

In the heart of Sri Lanka's rich cultural heritage lies a centuries-old tradition that has endured the test of time—traditional medicine and Ayurveda. This ancient system of healing, deeply rooted in the island's history, continues to be a source of wellness and rejuvenation for many.

Ayurveda, which translates to "the science of life," is a holistic system of medicine that originated in ancient India and found its way to Sri Lanka thousands of years ago. It is based on the fundamental principle that the balance of three vital energies, or "doshas" (Vata, Pitta, and Kapha), within the body is essential for health and well-being.

In Sri Lanka, Ayurveda has evolved into a unique form that incorporates indigenous medicinal plants and herbs, along with traditional healing practices passed down through generations. The island's tropical climate and biodiversity have endowed it with a wealth of botanical resources that form the cornerstone of Ayurvedic treatments.

One of the most distinctive features of Sri Lankan Ayurveda is the use of herbal preparations and oils for various therapeutic purposes. These preparations often include ingredients like cinnamon, ginger, turmeric, and a wide array of aromatic herbs. Many of these herbs are cultivated locally or wild-harvested from the island's lush forests.

Ayurvedic treatments in Sri Lanka are tailored to the individual's constitution, or "Prakriti," and their specific health needs. Whether you seek relief from a chronic condition or simply wish to rejuvenate your body and mind, Ayurvedic practitioners will customize treatments that may include herbal massages, steam baths, dietary advice, and meditation.

Traditional Sri Lankan medicine, known as "Deshiya Chikitsa," complements Ayurveda and offers its own unique approach to healing. It incorporates indigenous practices such as "Hela Wedakama," where medicinal plants and herbs are used in various forms, including pastes, infusions, and decoctions, to treat a wide range of ailments.

The integration of Ayurveda and traditional medicine into the country's healthcare system has made these practices accessible to a broad spectrum of the population. Sri Lanka boasts numerous Ayurvedic hospitals, wellness resorts, and clinics where travelers and locals alike can experience the benefits of these ancient healing traditions.

Sri Lankan traditional medicine and Ayurveda aren't just about treating ailments; they promote a holistic approach to health that encompasses physical, mental, and spiritual well-being. The emphasis on prevention, lifestyle, and natural remedies aligns with the island's ethos of harmony with nature.

Visitors to Sri Lanka often find solace and healing in these time-tested traditions, whether it's seeking relief from a specific ailment or simply wanting to rejuvenate their body and mind. The practices of Ayurveda and traditional medicine continue to thrive, providing a bridge between the island's ancient past and its vibrant present.

As you delve into the world of Sri Lankan traditional medicine and Ayurveda, you'll discover the profound wisdom and healing potential that have been cherished for generations. It's a testament to the enduring value of holistic well-being and the synergy between nature and human health.

# Daily Life and Etiquette in Sri Lanka

Stepping into the vibrant tapestry of daily life in Sri Lanka reveals a rich blend of tradition, culture, and hospitality. The island's people, known for their warmth and friendliness, follow customs and etiquette deeply rooted in their heritage.

**Greetings and Politeness:** In Sri Lanka, greetings are a significant part of social interactions. A traditional greeting involves placing one's hands together in a prayer-like gesture and saying "Ayubowan" (pronounced eye-you-boh-wan), which means "May you have a long life." It's a respectful way to welcome someone. It's also customary to bow slightly when greeting elders as a sign of respect.

**Attire:** Dress in Sri Lanka is typically modest and conservative. For women, it's common to wear saris or dresses that cover the shoulders and knees when visiting religious sites. Men often wear a shirt and trousers. While beach attire is acceptable at coastal resorts, it's respectful to cover up when leaving the beach.

**Footwear:** Before entering someone's home or a temple, it's customary to remove your shoes. You'll often see a pile of shoes near the entrance as a sign of respect. In temples, you may need to go barefoot or wear special shoe covers provided at the site.

**Visiting Homes:** Sri Lankans are known for their hospitality, and if you're invited to someone's home, it's polite to bring a small gift, such as fruit or sweets. Remove your shoes before entering and wait to be invited to sit.

When offered food or drink, it's customary to accept, even if you only take a small portion.

**Dining Etiquette:** When dining with locals, it's common to eat with your right hand, as the left hand is traditionally considered less clean. Wash your hands before and after a meal. If you're a guest, wait to be served and don't begin eating until your host signals to start.

**Temple Etiquette:** When visiting Buddhist temples, it's essential to show respect. Dress modestly, remove your shoes, and cover your shoulders and knees. Follow the lead of locals when it comes to rituals, like lighting incense or offering flowers.

**Respecting Elders:** Respect for elders is a fundamental aspect of Sri Lankan culture. Addressing elders with polite titles like "Uncle" or "Aunty" is common, even if they aren't related to you.

**Public Behavior:** Public displays of affection, such as hugging and kissing, are considered inappropriate. While alcohol is available and consumed in Sri Lanka, public drunkenness is frowned upon.

**Language:** The official languages of Sri Lanka are Sinhala and Tamil, but many people also speak English, especially in urban areas and among those in the tourism industry. Learning a few basic phrases in Sinhala or Tamil can be a gesture of goodwill and appreciated by the locals.

**Tipping:** Tipping is customary in Sri Lanka, especially in restaurants and for service providers. A 10% to 15% tip is considered appropriate.

**Time:** Sri Lankans operate on "island time," which can be more relaxed compared to Western standards. Punctuality is appreciated but not always strictly adhered to.

Navigating daily life in Sri Lanka is a rewarding experience filled with cultural insights and warm encounters. By respecting local customs and etiquette, you'll not only feel more at ease but also forge meaningful connections with the island's hospitable people.

# Transportation and Getting Around

Navigating the diverse landscapes of Sri Lanka requires an understanding of the transportation options available on this island nation. From bustling cities to serene rural areas, the modes of travel in Sri Lanka cater to a wide range of preferences and budgets.

**Road Travel:** The road network in Sri Lanka is extensive and well-maintained, making road travel one of the most common ways to get around. The primary mode of road transport is by bus. Buses range from public, brightly colored options to private buses with varying levels of comfort. While public buses are budget-friendly, private buses often offer more comfortable seating and air conditioning.

For those seeking more flexibility and privacy, hiring a car with a driver is a popular choice. It allows you to explore at your own pace and reach destinations that may not be easily accessible by public transportation. However, be prepared for diverse road conditions and traffic congestion, especially in major cities like Colombo.

Tuk-tuks, locally known as "three-wheelers," are a ubiquitous sight on Sri Lankan roads. They provide a convenient and relatively affordable way to travel short distances within cities. Negotiate the fare with the driver before starting your journey, as meters are not always used.

**Trains:** Sri Lanka boasts a picturesque train network that winds through scenic landscapes, including lush tea plantations and coastal vistas. The train journey from

Kandy to Ella is particularly renowned for its breathtaking views. Trains are categorized into classes, with first-class and observation carriages providing a more comfortable experience. However, even second and third-class carriages offer memorable journeys.

It's advisable to book train tickets in advance, especially during the peak tourist season, as popular routes can fill up quickly. Be prepared for delays, as punctuality is not always guaranteed.

**Domestic Flights:** For those looking to cover longer distances quickly, domestic flights are available. Sri Lanka has several airports, including Bandaranaike International Airport in Colombo and regional airports in cities like Kandy and Jaffna. Domestic airlines offer regular flights to various destinations across the island.

**Ferries and Boats:** Given Sri Lanka's extensive coastline and numerous islands, ferries and boats play a significant role in transportation. From Colombo, you can take a ferry to places like Negombo and Kalpitiya. Additionally, boat tours and fishing excursions are popular activities in coastal areas.

**Cycling and Walking:** In more laid-back settings, such as rural villages and historic towns, cycling and walking are enjoyable ways to explore. Many tourist destinations offer bicycle rentals, allowing you to meander through picturesque landscapes and immerse yourself in local culture.

**Local Insights:** When traveling within Sri Lanka, it's essential to consider local customs and norms. Dress modestly, especially when visiting religious sites. Always remove your shoes before entering someone's home or a temple. When using public transportation, be prepared for crowded buses and trains during peak hours.

Sri Lanka's transportation options cater to a variety of traveler preferences. Whether you're seeking the scenic route by train, the convenience of road travel, or the speed of domestic flights, you'll find a way to explore this beautiful island and all it has to offer.

# Exploring the Coastal Gems: Mirissa, Unawatuna, and More

As the sun casts its golden glow upon the Indian Ocean, the coastal towns of Mirissa and Unawatuna beckon travelers with their picturesque shores, vibrant marine life, and a laid-back atmosphere that epitomizes the essence of Sri Lanka's southern coast.

**Mirissa:** Nestled on the southern tip of Sri Lanka, Mirissa has emerged as a sought-after destination for beach lovers and whale watchers alike. This tranquil coastal town, known for its serene beaches, is the gateway to unforgettable adventures on the high seas.

Mirissa's beaches are postcard-perfect, with palm-fringed shores and gentle waves. Whether you're a sun worshiper seeking the perfect tan or a surfer catching the waves, Mirissa has something for everyone. Its relaxed ambiance and charming beachfront cafés create an ideal setting for relaxation and introspection.

One of Mirissa's most notable attractions is its prominence as a whale-watching hub. Excursions set sail from the harbor in search of these majestic creatures that grace the waters of the Indian Ocean. Blue whales, sperm whales, and playful dolphins are often spotted during these expeditions, offering an awe-inspiring glimpse into the marine world.

Mirissa's nightlife is as vibrant as its beaches are tranquil. The town comes alive after dark, with beach parties, seafood feasts, and music wafting through the night air. It's a chance to savor fresh seafood delicacies while swaying to the rhythms of island beats.

**Unawatuna:** A short drive eastward along the southern coast brings you to the enchanting shores of Unawatuna. This charming coastal town is renowned for its crescent-shaped bay, which boasts calm and crystal-clear waters—an ideal spot for swimming and snorkeling.

Unawatuna's coral reef, protected within a marine sanctuary, offers a stunning underwater world to explore. Snorkelers and divers can encounter vibrant coral formations and an array of marine life, from colorful fish to graceful sea turtles.

For history enthusiasts, a visit to the Japanese Peace Pagoda is a must. This serene temple, perched atop a hill, provides panoramic views of the coastline and the Indian Ocean. It's a tranquil place for reflection and a glimpse into Sri Lanka's spiritual heritage.

The relaxed pace of life in Unawatuna is complemented by beachside dining, where you can savor fresh seafood and international cuisines while watching the sunset paint the sky in shades of orange and pink.

**Beyond Mirissa and Unawatuna:** The coastal gems of Mirissa and Unawatuna are just the beginning of your southern Sri Lankan journey. Nearby attractions like Weligama, known for its stilt fishermen, and Galle, with its UNESCO-listed fort, offer further exploration opportunities.

As you explore these coastal wonders, you'll find that Mirissa, Unawatuna, and their neighboring towns encapsulate the magic of Sri Lanka's southern coastline. Whether you're seeking adventure on the water, tranquility on the beach, or cultural immersion in historic locales, the southern coast has it all, inviting you to discover its unique charm and natural beauty.

# Water Sports and Adventure Activities

Sri Lanka, with its stunning coastline, lush interior, and diverse terrain, is a playground for adventure seekers and water sports enthusiasts. From surfing to diving, trekking to white-water rafting, this island nation offers a plethora of adrenaline-pumping activities to suit every taste.

**Surfing:** The southern and eastern coasts of Sri Lanka are renowned for their consistent waves, making it a surfer's paradise. Spots like Arugam Bay on the east coast and Weligama on the south coast attract surfers from around the world. Whether you're a beginner looking for lessons or an experienced surfer chasing epic breaks, Sri Lanka has waves for everyone.

**Scuba Diving and Snorkeling:** Sri Lanka's crystal-clear waters are home to vibrant coral reefs and an abundance of marine life. Popular diving spots include Hikkaduwa, Unawatuna, and Trincomalee, where you can explore colorful coral gardens and encounter reef fish, turtles, and even shipwrecks. For a more relaxed underwater experience, snorkeling is a fantastic option, allowing you to observe marine life in shallow, easily accessible areas.

**Whale Watching:** Mirissa, on the southern coast, is famous for whale watching expeditions. The deep waters off Mirissa are frequented by blue whales, the largest animals on Earth, as well as sperm whales and playful dolphins. These excursions offer a chance to witness these magnificent creatures in their natural habitat. **White-Water Rafting:** For thrill-seekers, the Kelani River in Kitulgala provides an adrenaline rush with its white-water rafting adventures. Surrounded by lush rainforests, this river offers a heart-pounding journey through rapids of varying difficulty levels. It's a memorable way to experience the island's interior and natural beauty.

**Trekking and Hiking:** Sri Lanka's interior is a hiker's dream. The central highlands, including destinations like Ella and Horton Plains National Park, offer scenic trekking routes through tea plantations, cloud forests, and mist-covered peaks. The trek to World's End in Horton Plains is particularly popular, rewarding hikers with panoramic views.

**Cycling:** Exploring Sri Lanka on two wheels is an excellent way to connect with the local culture and environment. Whether you're cycling through ancient cities like Anuradhapura or pedaling along the coastal roads, the island offers diverse landscapes to explore by bike.

**Wildlife Safaris:** Venture into the heart of Sri Lanka's national parks for a chance to spot diverse wildlife. Yala National Park is famous for its leopard population, while Minneriya National Park hosts the "Gathering," a spectacular congregation of elephants. Wilpattu National Park is known for its remote and wild landscapes.

**Zip-Lining and Canyoning:** For a dose of adventure with a view, zip-lining through rainforests and canyoning down waterfalls in places like Kitulgala offer exhilarating experiences that blend nature and adventure seamlessly.

Sri Lanka's diverse landscapes provide an adventure playground for those seeking outdoor thrills and water sports. Whether you're riding the waves, exploring underwater worlds, or trekking through pristine forests, the island's natural beauty and warm hospitality make it a top destination for adventure enthusiasts from around the globe.

# Ayurvedic Spas and Wellness Retreats

In the heart of Sri Lanka's rich cultural tapestry lies a treasure trove of wellness traditions dating back thousands of years. Ayurveda, often referred to as the "science of life," is a holistic system of healing that harmonizes the body, mind, and spirit. Sri Lanka, with its deep-rooted Ayurvedic heritage, offers a haven for those seeking rejuvenation and holistic well-being.

**The Essence of Ayurveda:** Ayurveda, originating from ancient India, has been an integral part of Sri Lankan culture for centuries. It revolves around the balance of the three doshas—Vata, Pitta, and Kapha—in one's body, which are believed to govern various physical and mental aspects. Ayurvedic treatments and therapies aim to restore this balance, promoting vitality and longevity.

**Ayurvedic Spas and Retreats:** Sri Lanka boasts a multitude of Ayurvedic spas and wellness retreats, each offering a unique blend of traditional wisdom and modern comforts. These retreats are often nestled in lush natural settings, providing a serene and tranquil atmosphere conducive to healing.

**Ayurvedic Treatments:** Visitors to Ayurvedic retreats can undergo a personalized assessment by Ayurvedic physicians who determine their dosha constitution and any imbalances. Based on this assessment, a tailored treatment plan is created, encompassing a range of therapies such as:

- **Panchakarma:** A deep cleansing and detoxification process that includes various treatments like herbal oil massages, steam baths, and enemas.
- **Abhyanga:** A soothing full-body oil massage that promotes relaxation and improved circulation.
- **Shirodhara:** A therapy where warm herbal oil is gently poured over the forehead, known for its calming effects on the nervous system.
- **Herbal Steam Baths:** A rejuvenating therapy that detoxifies the body through the use of herbal-infused steam.

These treatments are designed to address specific health concerns, alleviate stress, improve sleep quality, and enhance overall vitality.

**Yoga and Meditation:** Many Ayurvedic retreats in Sri Lanka incorporate yoga and meditation into their wellness programs. Yoga helps to harmonize the body and mind, while meditation fosters inner peace and mental clarity. Together, they complement Ayurvedic treatments, promoting holistic well-being.

**Healthy Cuisine:** Ayurvedic retreats also emphasize the importance of diet in maintaining a balanced and healthy life. Guests are typically served Ayurvedic meals that align with their dosha constitution and treatment plan. These meals are not only nourishing but also flavorful, showcasing the culinary richness of Ayurvedic cuisine.

**The Holistic Experience:** Beyond physical treatments, Ayurvedic retreats encourage guests to immerse themselves in the healing power of nature. Sri Lanka's lush landscapes, serene beaches, and tropical forests provide the ideal backdrop for relaxation and rejuvenation.

In conclusion, Ayurvedic spas and wellness retreats in Sri Lanka offer a profound journey of self-discovery and healing. Rooted in ancient wisdom and set in picturesque surroundings, these retreats provide a holistic approach to well-being, inviting travelers to experience the transformative power of Ayurveda and return home with a renewed sense of vitality and balance.

# Shopping for Souvenirs and Handicrafts

Exploring the vibrant markets and boutiques of Sri Lanka is a delightful journey into a world of artistry and craftsmanship. The island, with its rich cultural heritage and diverse landscapes, has cultivated a wide array of unique souvenirs and handicrafts that reflect its history and traditions.

**Handwoven Textiles:** One of the most iconic Sri Lankan handicrafts is handwoven textiles, including the renowned saris and sarongs. These intricate fabrics often feature vibrant colors and intricate designs, showcasing the skill of local weavers. You can find them in local markets or visit weaving villages to witness the age-old craft in action.

**Wooden and Brass Carvings:** Sri Lanka's wood and brass carvings are exquisite examples of artisanal skill. Intricately carved masks, figurines, and furniture adorn markets and shops, making for unique and culturally rich souvenirs. The ancient city of Kandy is particularly famous for its traditional wood and brass craftsmanship.

**Gemstones and Jewelry:** Known as the "Gem Island," Sri Lanka is celebrated for its precious and semi-precious gemstones, including sapphires, rubies, and moonstones. Colombo and Ratnapura are major hubs for gemstone shopping. These gems are skillfully incorporated into beautiful jewelry pieces that make for stunning souvenirs.

**Batik Art:** Batik is a traditional Sri Lankan art form that involves wax-resist dyeing on fabric. The result is vibrant, colorful textiles featuring intricate patterns and designs. Batik clothing, wall hangings, and accessories are popular choices for tourists seeking unique mementos.

**Pottery and Ceramics:** From traditional clay pots to intricately glazed ceramic pieces, Sri Lanka offers a wide range of pottery and ceramics. Visit the town of Matale to witness pottery-making firsthand, or explore boutiques for decorative and functional ceramic items.

**Masks:** Traditional masks, often used in Sri Lankan dance and drama, are captivating souvenirs. The masks, with their exaggerated expressions and intricate designs, carry cultural significance. Ambalangoda is a renowned center for mask production and sales.

**Spices and Ayurvedic Products:** Sri Lanka's spices are famous for their quality and flavor. Visitors can purchase an array of spices like cinnamon, cardamom, and cloves, along with Ayurvedic products such as herbal oils and beauty remedies, providing a taste of the island's healing traditions.

**Tea and Tea-Related Products:** Sri Lanka is globally recognized for its tea, and a visit to the island wouldn't be complete without indulging in the world-famous Ceylon tea. You can explore tea estates and purchase a variety of teas, from single-origin to flavored blends. Tea-related products like tea sets and infusers also make for excellent souvenirs.

**Lacquerware:** Lacquerware, often found in the coastal city of Galle, features intricate designs on wooden or brass objects coated with lacquer. It's a unique and visually stunning handicraft that represents a blend of local and colonial influences.

**Antiques and Collectibles:** For avid collectors, Sri Lanka offers antique shops and markets where you can find unique pieces of history, including old coins, colonial-era furniture, and vintage items.

**Remembering Sri Lanka:** Shopping for souvenirs and handicrafts in Sri Lanka is not just about acquiring material possessions; it's a way of preserving memories and immersing yourself in the island's rich culture. Each item tells a story of artistry and tradition, allowing you to take home a piece of Sri Lanka's unique charm and heritage.

# Tea Tasting and Plantation Tours

Sri Lanka, formerly known as Ceylon, is synonymous with tea. Its lush hill country, with its mist-covered mountains and terraced tea plantations, is the birthplace of Ceylon tea, renowned for its exceptional flavor and quality. Exploring the world of tea in Sri Lanka is a sensory journey that unveils the artistry and heritage of this beloved beverage.

**The Ceylon Tea Story:** Sri Lanka's tea industry has a fascinating history dating back to the 19th century when British planters introduced tea cultivation. Today, the island ranks among the world's top tea producers and exporters. The industry's growth has been driven by the favorable climate, fertile soil, and skilled workforce.

**Tea Plantations:** The central highlands of Sri Lanka, including regions like Nuwara Eliya, Kandy, and Ella, are carpeted with emerald-green tea estates. These picturesque landscapes offer more than just stunning views; they provide an opportunity to witness tea cultivation up close. The sight of tea pickers meticulously plucking the tender tea leaves is a common scene in these regions.

**Tea Varieties:** Sri Lanka produces an array of tea varieties, each with its distinct flavor profile. The main types of Ceylon tea include:

- **Black Tea:** The most common and popular variety, known for its robust flavor and versatility.
- **Green Tea:** Lighter in flavor and color, green tea offers a more delicate taste.

- **White Tea:** A rare and prized variety, white tea is made from young tea buds and has a subtle, sweet flavor.
- **Herbal Teas:** Sri Lanka also produces a range of herbal infusions, including cinnamon tea, lemongrass tea, and spice blends.

**Tea Tasting:** No visit to a tea plantation is complete without a tea tasting experience. Tea factories and estate bungalows offer guided tastings where you can sample a variety of teas while learning about the nuances of each. Professional tasters will walk you through the art of tea appreciation, from observing the dry leaves to savoring the brewed infusion.

**Tea and Tourism:** Sri Lanka's tea industry has seamlessly integrated with tourism. Many tea estates open their doors to visitors, offering guided plantation tours. These tours provide insights into the tea-making process, from plucking and withering to rolling and fermentation. You'll also have the chance to witness the machinery used in tea production.

**Tea Trails:** For those seeking an immersive tea experience, boutique hotels and bungalows in the heart of tea country offer tea-themed stays. These accommodations provide not only comfortable lodgings but also opportunities for guided treks through the plantations, tea plucking sessions, and private tea tastings.

**Tea and Culture:** Tea has become an integral part of Sri Lankan culture. The daily ritual of enjoying a cup of tea, often accompanied by snacks like "short eats," is deeply ingrained in the lifestyle. Visiting local teahouses and enjoying a cup of freshly brewed Ceylon tea with the locals is a delightful way to connect with the island's culture.

In essence, tea tasting and plantation tours in Sri Lanka are a window into the heritage and craftsmanship behind one of the world's most cherished beverages. It's a journey that engages your senses, deepens your appreciation for tea, and allows you to savor the authentic flavors of Ceylon.

# Discovering Sri Lanka's Hidden Gems

Sri Lanka, a land of boundless beauty and cultural richness, offers a treasure trove of hidden gems that beckon intrepid travelers. Beyond its renowned attractions, this island nation harbors secrets waiting to be uncovered, revealing a side of Sri Lanka that few have the privilege to explore.

**1. Jungle Beach, Unawatuna:** Nestled away from the bustling beaches of Unawatuna, Jungle Beach is a secluded paradise accessible by a short hike through a lush forest. Its pristine shores, crystal-clear waters, and tranquil ambiance make it a haven for those seeking solitude and natural beauty.

**2. Mannar Island:** Located in the northern part of Sri Lanka, Mannar Island is an off-the-beaten-path destination. It's known for its serene beaches, ancient baobab trees, and the iconic Mannar Fort, which offers panoramic views of the surrounding landscape.

**3. The Rock Temple, Trincomalee:** While Trincomalee is famous for its beaches, the lesser-known Rock Temple is a hidden gem worth exploring. Carved into a massive boulder, this ancient temple is adorned with intricate sculptures and provides a glimpse into Sri Lanka's rich history.

**4. Pidurangala Rock, Sigiriya:** Most visitors flock to the iconic Sigiriya Rock, but nearby Pidurangala Rock offers a unique perspective. Climbing Pidurangala rewards you with a breathtaking panoramic view of Sigiriya and the surrounding countryside, making it a photographer's dream.

**5. Kalpitiya Peninsula:** For water sports enthusiasts and nature lovers, Kalpitiya Peninsula is a revelation. This pristine coastal area is a hotspot for kitesurfing, dolphin watching, and exploring the lush Wilpattu National Park.

**6. Delft Island:** Stepping onto Delft Island feels like entering a different world. Located in the Gulf of Mannar, this island boasts a distinct Dutch colonial heritage, evident in its coral walls and quaint village life. It's also famous for its wild ponies and coral-strewn beaches.

**7. Horton Plains National Park:** Nestled in Sri Lanka's central highlands, Horton Plains is a UNESCO World Heritage Site known for its dramatic landscapes. The highlight is World's End, a sheer cliff with a drop of nearly 1,000 meters, offering a breathtaking view of the plains below.

**8. Lankatilaka Temple, Kandy:** While the Temple of the Tooth Relic is Kandy's main attraction, the nearby Lankatilaka Temple is often overlooked. This 14th-century temple features stunning architecture and intricate murals, making it a hidden gem for history and art enthusiasts.

**9. Madu River Safari:** Exploring the Madu River by boat is a serene and lesser-known experience. The river meanders through mangrove forests, revealing hidden islands and abundant birdlife. It's a peaceful escape from the more touristy spots.

**10. Belilena Cave, Kitulgala:** For adventure seekers and history buffs, the Belilena Cave in Kitulgala is an intriguing find. This cave is famous for its prehistoric archaeological discoveries, including ancient tools and skeletal remains of Homo sapiens.

Unearthing these hidden gems of Sri Lanka requires a sense of adventure and a willingness to stray from the beaten path. Each of these lesser-known destinations offers a unique insight into the diverse and captivating tapestry of this enchanting island, making your journey all the more memorable.

# Off the Beaten Path: Lesser-Known Destinations

As you embark on your journey through Sri Lanka, there's an exciting world beyond the well-trodden tourist routes. These lesser-known destinations offer a unique glimpse into the soul of this captivating island, away from the crowds and commercialization.

**1. Mannar Island:** Tucked away in the northern reaches of Sri Lanka, Mannar Island is a hidden treasure. Its pristine beaches, ancient baobab trees, and the historic Mannar Fort are a testament to its charm. The island's tranquil ambiance provides an ideal escape from the bustle of more touristy spots.

**2. Kalpitiya Peninsula:** For adventure seekers and nature lovers, Kalpitiya Peninsula is a revelation. This coastal area is a haven for kitesurfing enthusiasts, with strong winds and flat waters creating the perfect conditions. The peninsula is also a prime spot for dolphin watching, and the nearby Wilpattu National Park offers a chance to spot Sri Lanka's incredible wildlife.

**3. Jaffna Peninsula:** In the far north of Sri Lanka lies the Jaffna Peninsula, a region steeped in history and culture. It's home to unique Tamil traditions, and its iconic Jaffna Fort, Nagadeepa Vihara, and Keerimalai natural springs offer a glimpse into its rich heritage.

**4. The Rock Temple, Trincomalee:** While Trincomalee is famous for its beaches, the lesser-known Rock Temple is a hidden gem worth exploring. Carved into a massive boulder, this ancient temple is adorned with intricate sculptures and provides a glimpse into Sri Lanka's rich history.

**5. Delft Island:** Delft Island, located in the Gulf of Mannar, feels like stepping back in time. Its coral walls, quaint village life, and wild ponies reflect its Dutch colonial history. The island's coral-strewn beaches and serene atmosphere offer a truly unique escape.

**6. Horton Plains National Park:** For nature enthusiasts, Horton Plains National Park is a must-visit. This UNESCO World Heritage Site is located in the central highlands and is known for its dramatic landscapes, including the famous World's End, a sheer cliff with a stunning view.

**7. Lankatilaka Temple, Kandy:** While Kandy's Temple of the Tooth Relic is a popular attraction, the nearby Lankatilaka Temple is often overlooked. This 14th-century temple features stunning architecture and intricate murals, making it a hidden gem for history and art enthusiasts.

**8. Madu River Safari:** The Madu River offers a serene and lesser-known experience. Explore it by boat as you navigate through mangrove forests, discovering hidden islands and abundant birdlife. It's a peaceful escape from more crowded attractions.

**9. Belilena Cave, Kitulgala:** For those with a taste for adventure and history, the Belilena Cave in Kitulgala is an intriguing find. It's famous for its prehistoric archaeological discoveries, including ancient tools and skeletal remains of Homo sapiens.

These lesser-known destinations in Sri Lanka beckon with their untamed beauty, historical significance, and unique cultural experiences. Venturing off the beaten path rewards you with an authentic and enriching journey, allowing you to connect with the heart and soul of this diverse island nation.

# The Impact of Tsunami and Post-Disaster Recovery

In the early morning hours of December 26, 2004, a catastrophic event unfolded along the coastlines of several countries bordering the Indian Ocean. A powerful undersea earthquake, registering a magnitude of 9.1-9.3 off the west coast of northern Sumatra, triggered a series of tsunamis that raced across the ocean at remarkable speeds. When these massive waves reached the shores of Sri Lanka, they unleashed unimaginable devastation, leaving an indelible mark on the nation's history.

The impact of the 2004 Indian Ocean tsunami on Sri Lanka was profound, both in terms of loss and recovery. The tsunami waves struck with little warning, catching coastal communities off guard and resulting in widespread destruction. Thousands of lives were tragically lost, and countless homes, businesses, and infrastructure were washed away in a matter of minutes.

The aftermath of the disaster prompted an immediate and massive humanitarian response, with aid pouring in from around the world. The Sri Lankan government, alongside numerous international organizations and volunteers, launched relief efforts to provide emergency assistance to survivors, including food, clean water, shelter, and medical care.

In the years that followed, the focus shifted from emergency relief to long-term recovery and reconstruction. The challenges were immense, as Sri Lanka faced the daunting task of rebuilding not only its physical infrastructure but also the lives and livelihoods of those affected. Communities along the coastline were forever altered, with many fishermen losing their boats and equipment, and families grappling with the loss of loved ones.

Despite the enormity of the task, Sri Lanka demonstrated resilience and determination in its recovery efforts. International aid played a crucial role in rebuilding coastal communities, rehabilitating schools, and constructing safer shelters. Efforts were also made to establish early warning systems and disaster preparedness programs to mitigate the impact of future natural disasters.

The tragedy of the 2004 tsunami underscored the importance of disaster preparedness and international cooperation in responding to such events. It also highlighted the resilience of the Sri Lankan people, who, with the support of the global community, were able to rebuild their lives and communities.

The impact of the tsunami on Sri Lanka serves as a poignant reminder of the fragility of life and the need for vigilance in the face of natural disasters. It is a testament to the strength of the human spirit and the capacity for recovery and renewal in the wake of tragedy. Sri Lanka's post-disaster recovery is a testament to the nation's resilience and the power of collective efforts in the face of adversity.

# Sustainable Tourism in Sri Lanka

Sri Lanka, with its breathtaking landscapes, rich cultural heritage, and diverse wildlife, has long been a popular destination for travelers seeking natural beauty and cultural immersion. However, as the world becomes increasingly conscious of the environmental and social impact of tourism, Sri Lanka has recognized the importance of sustainable tourism practices to preserve its natural wonders and support local communities.

One of the key initiatives in promoting sustainable tourism in Sri Lanka is the emphasis on responsible travel. Travelers are encouraged to respect local customs, protect the environment, and support the livelihoods of local communities. By engaging in eco-friendly activities and choosing accommodations that prioritize sustainability, tourists can minimize their impact on the environment.

The protection of Sri Lanka's national parks and wildlife reserves is another crucial aspect of sustainable tourism. Sri Lanka boasts a remarkable array of biodiversity, including elephants, leopards, and a multitude of bird species. Efforts have been made to implement responsible wildlife viewing practices, ensuring that animals are not disturbed or harmed by tourism activities.

The island nation also places importance on preserving its cultural heritage. Many ancient sites and temples are UNESCO World Heritage Sites, and strict regulations are in place to protect these historical treasures. Visitors are encouraged to explore these sites with respect for their historical and religious significance.

The concept of sustainable tourism extends to the accommodation sector as well. Eco-friendly resorts and lodges have emerged, focusing on minimizing energy consumption, reducing waste, and supporting local communities. These establishments often integrate with the natural surroundings, offering guests a chance to immerse themselves in the beauty of Sri Lanka's landscapes.

Community-based tourism initiatives are gaining momentum, allowing travelers to engage with local communities and learn about their traditions and ways of life. This not only provides a more authentic travel experience but also contributes to the economic well-being of rural communities.

Sri Lanka has also made significant strides in waste management and recycling practices in popular tourist areas. Efforts have been made to reduce single-use plastics, and visitors are encouraged to bring reusable water bottles and bags to minimize plastic waste.

The country's commitment to sustainable tourism is further exemplified by its dedication to protecting marine life and coral reefs. Coral conservation projects and strict regulations on activities like snorkeling and diving help safeguard the fragile underwater ecosystems.

In recent years, Sri Lanka has positioned itself as a global leader in sustainable tourism, receiving accolades and recognition for its efforts to balance tourism growth with environmental and cultural preservation. By embracing the principles of responsible and sustainable tourism, Sri Lanka is not only safeguarding its natural and cultural heritage but also offering travelers a more meaningful and authentic experience on this enchanting island.

# Practical Travel Tips and Advice

Traveling to Sri Lanka, with its diverse landscapes, rich culture, and warm hospitality, is a memorable experience. To make the most of your journey and ensure a smooth visit, consider these practical travel tips and advice:

1. **Visa Requirements:** Before traveling to Sri Lanka, check the visa requirements for your country. Most travelers can obtain an Electronic Travel Authorization (ETA) online or upon arrival at the airport. Ensure your passport has at least six months of validity from your planned departure date.

2. **Health Precautions:** Consult your healthcare provider about necessary vaccinations and health precautions for Sri Lanka. Carry any prescribed medications with you and have a basic first-aid kit.

3. **Currency:** The currency in Sri Lanka is the Sri Lankan Rupee (LKR). ATMs are widely available, especially in urban areas. Inform your bank about your travel plans to avoid any issues with card transactions.

4. **Language:** Sinhala and Tamil are the official languages, but English is widely spoken and understood in tourist areas. Learning a few local phrases can enhance your experience.

5. **Weather:** Sri Lanka has a tropical climate, so pack lightweight clothing. However, if you plan to visit the hill country, where temperatures are cooler, bring some warm clothing.

6. **Travel Insurance:** It's advisable to have comprehensive travel insurance that covers medical emergencies, trip cancellations, and lost luggage.

7. **Transportation:** Sri Lanka offers various transportation options. Trains are scenic and affordable, while buses are economical but can be crowded. Tuk-tuks are a convenient way to explore cities and towns. For longer distances, consider domestic flights.

8. **Safety:** Sri Lanka is generally safe for travelers. However, exercise common-sense precautions, like safeguarding your belongings and avoiding isolated areas at night.

9. **Local Cuisine:** Sri Lankan cuisine is flavorful and diverse. Don't miss trying traditional dishes like rice and curry, hoppers, and kottu roti. Be cautious with spicy food if you're not used to it.

10. **Cultural Respect:** Sri Lanka has a rich cultural heritage. When visiting temples, cover your shoulders and knees, remove your shoes, and show respect for local customs and traditions.

11. **Electrical Outlets:** The standard voltage is 230V, and the frequency is 50Hz. Sri Lanka uses Type D and Type G plug sockets. Bring the appropriate adapters and voltage converters if needed.

12. **Internet and Connectivity:** SIM cards with data plans are readily available, providing affordable internet access. Many hotels and cafes also offer Wi-Fi.

13. **Local Etiquette:** Sri Lankans are known for their warmth and friendliness. Greet with a smile, and be polite and respectful. Bargaining is common in markets but do so respectfully.

14. **Exploring Wildlife:** If you plan to visit national parks, follow the guidelines for wildlife viewing. Maintain a safe distance from animals and never feed them.

15. **Environmental Responsibility:** Support sustainable tourism by minimizing your environmental footprint. Dispose of trash responsibly and avoid single-use plastics.
16. **Emergency Contacts:** Save important numbers like the local police, medical facilities, and your country's embassy or consulate in case of emergencies.

These practical travel tips and advice will help you make the most of your journey through Sri Lanka, ensuring a safe and enjoyable experience in this enchanting island nation.

# Epilogue

As we conclude our journey through the vibrant tapestry of Sri Lanka, it's time to reflect on the myriad experiences and wonders that this island nation has to offer. From its lush rainforests to its golden beaches, from its ancient temples to its bustling cities, Sri Lanka has captivated travelers for centuries.

Throughout our exploration, we've delved into the island's rich history, spanning from its ancient civilizations to the colonial era, and witnessed its journey to modernity as an independent nation. We've marveled at its geographical wonders, from the majestic mountains of the hill country to the pristine coral reefs of its coastal waters.

The diverse and welcoming people of Sri Lanka, with their distinct languages, religions, and traditions, have added depth to our understanding of this remarkable place. We've learned about the significance of the Temple of the Tooth Relic, the spirituality that permeates the island, and the vibrant festivals that bring communities together in celebration.

We've savored the flavors of Sri Lankan cuisine, with its spicy curries, aromatic rice dishes, and tropical fruits. We've explored the arts and crafts of the island, from intricate woodwork to vibrant batik textiles, and been mesmerized by its traditional music and dance forms. As we've traversed this land, we've encountered its astonishing wildlife, including the elusive leopards of Yala National Park and the gentle giants of the elephant sanctuaries. We've also glimpsed the urgent need for conservation efforts to protect these treasures for future generations.

Sri Lanka's breathtaking beaches, whether in Mirissa or Unawatuna, have offered moments of tranquility and exhilaration, while its enchanting hill country and tea plantations have provided a glimpse into a world of verdant beauty and history.

We've explored ancient cities and historical sites, climbed the iconic Sigiriya Rock Fortress, and marveled at the frescoes in the cave temples of Dambulla. We've walked the living fort of Galle, a testament to the island's colonial history, and wandered the bustling streets of Colombo, the capital city.

Venturing north to Jaffna, we discovered a lesser-explored gem, and explored the sacred city of Anuradhapura, a UNESCO World Heritage Site. We journeyed through the medieval capital of Polonnaruwa, each step taking us deeper into the island's past.

Now, as we reach the epilogue of this journey, it's a reminder that while our words can paint a vivid picture, there is no substitute for experiencing Sri Lanka firsthand. Its magic lies not just in its natural beauty and historical grandeur but also in the warmth and hospitality of its people.

Sri Lanka is a place where traditions meet modernity, where serenity meets adventure, and where history meets the future. It's a land that leaves an indelible mark on all who visit, a place where every traveler finds their unique connection.

As we bid farewell to Sri Lanka, may your own journey to this island of wonders be filled with discovery, enlightenment, and lasting memories. And as you close the pages of this book, know that the story of Sri Lanka, with all its splendor and complexity, continues to unfold, waiting for you to be a part of it.

Printed in Great Britain
by Amazon